Roly Bain was born in London in 1954, one of the triplet children of Richard Findlater, the biographer of the first great English clown, Joe Grimaldi, and at the age of eight decided to become a clown himself.

He was educated at St Paul's School, later studied theology at Bristol University, and was ordained in 1978, becoming curate in Catford, succentor at Southwark Cathedral, and then vicar in Tooting.

In 1982 Roly helped found *Holy Fools*, a loose-knit network of people committed to clowning in ministry and worship. In 1990 he resigned his living, spent a year at Fool Time, the circus school in Bristol, and has been clowning full-time ever since.

Roly is Honorary Curate at the Clowns' Church in Dalston, East London, as well as Chaplain to Clowns International, and has won several awards, including Clown of the Year in 1994, and the Clowns International Slapstick Award in 1999. He travels over 30,000 miles a year visiting schools, hospitals, churches, prisons and all places where people gather, both in Britain and elsewhere, and his work is now supported by the Faith and Foolishness Trust.

He is married to Jane and they have two sons, Jack and Sam.

Playing the Fool

Roly Bain

CANTERBURY
PRESS
Norwich

Text © Roly Bain 2001

First published in 2001 by The Canterbury Press Norwich
(a publishing imprint of Hymns Ancient & Modern Limited,
a registered charity)
St Mary's Works, St Mary's Plain
Norwich, Norfolk NR3 3BH

Roly Bain has asserted his right under the
Copyright, Design and Patents Act, 1988, to be
identified as the Author of this Work

British Library Cataloguing in Publication data

A catalogue record of this book is available
from the British Library

ISBN 1 85311 439 1

Typeset by Rowland Phototypesetting Ltd,
Bury St Edmunds, Suffolk
Printed and bound in Great Britain by
Bookmarque Ltd, Croydon, Surrey

Dedicated to my late
father, Richard Findlater

Contents

Childish Things

I am a triplet – there are three of me! When it came to celebrating our fortieth birthday we decided not only to have a big party but to put up an exhibition of photographs of the three of us covering as many of those forty years as we could manage. My sister Jennie probably had the most photographs but it was brother Toby who surprised us all. He is an accountant and thus a little lacking in imagination, and he had stashed away a box of old photographs that had belonged to our late father without even looking at them. He produced this treasure trove of photos that none of us had ever seen before, but the real treasure was to be found in our old schoolbooks which Dad had saved and put at the bottom of the box. There were two exercise books belonging to each of us from our primary school years at Sheen Mount, a school we'd left at the age of eight. I flicked through my Composition book with its myriad corny tales in my large and rounded eight-year-old joined-up writing, and there, written on 30 January 1962, two weeks after our eighth birthday, was my childhood ambition literally writ large:

> When I grow up I want to be a clown like Coco. The circus I want to go to is Bertram Mills Circus. I am going to wear special clothes and make-up. I am going to have a big red mouth and a big round red nose. My

face is going to be white, with little bits of wool for hair. I have already thought of an act. It is called the broken mirror act. This is how you do it. I have a broken mirror and I look through it. Behind the mirror is a monkey and I say I need a haircut everywhere. Do you see the joke? Well I pretend that the monkey is me. I hope it will work. I want to be a clown because I think it is exciting to be one. The way I get in is this. I ask all the circuses if they want me, and the one that wants me then I go to that circus. I don't want to earn any money either. If I do get any money I am going to buy more things and give the rest to the poor. I am also going to hospitals to make the patients laugh and make them feel better.

Little did the eight-year-old me know that I would end up fulfilling that childhood ambition. While I've never worked for a circus, I've performed in big tops and indeed in most places that you can think of. I do find it very exciting. I've never performed with a monkey, but the mirror gag is a classic circus clown routine. I'm glad to say that my make-up is very different to the one envisaged. I have a Larson cartoon hanging on the wall of my downstairs lavatory, with a bunch of Mafia hoodlums surrounding a clown with a big red mouth and a big red nose who is tied to a chair in the midst of them, and the caption reads, 'The first thing I'm gonna do is wipe that smile off your face'! That sums up my view of clown make-up. I wear very little make-up, though I do have a grease-painted red nose. I have been to hospitals and indeed now do so regularly – how enlightened of an eight-year-old to dream of that. Clowns have visited hospitals for a long time now. Coco did a lot of it. But it's only in the last few years that it has become quite so established as a place where clowns belong. But I fear I'm not as altruistic as I obviously once was because I am a full-time clown with a family, who needs to pay the bills! But more of all later . . .

There is so much that I am grateful to my father for because it was he who fostered those early hopes and dreams. He always took us to the circus. In the late 1950s and early 1960s, Bertram Mills Circus at Olympia in London was the big event at Christmas – it was my Advent because when I went to Bertram Mills I knew that Christmas was coming. My parents divorced when I was seven so we had holidays in the summer with Dad. If there was a travelling circus, we'd go. At one little circus in Sussex I remember having my hair dressed by a clown with an enormous comb. I was in a state of great excitement as he climbed the bleachers to reach me and carefully but gleefully parted my hair in the wrong direction. The summer after my school composition about clowns we had a holiday in a caravan near Salcombe in Devon, and I had read Coco's autobiography – quite an achievement for an eight-year-old! I promptly sat down in the caravan window, drew a picture of my ideal clown, and wrote underneath it, 'I want to be a clown'. I remember doing it even now. My mother sent me the picture years later and I stored it somewhere very safe – and have never seen it since! But Dad was into clowns too. He wrote the biography of Grimaldi, the first great English clown, who was also the first to wear clown's greasepaint as we know it today. In my twenties Dad and I started to collect clown figures. He had photographs of Grock, the great Swiss clown, on his study wall, and books on clowns too, which is why I had access to the Coco autobiography. That now sits on my shelves together with many others, but it was his books that started me off. I have to admit also that the downstairs lavatory mentioned above is also festooned with pictures of Grock, and a wonderful picture of Grock hangs above the desk in my study.

So clowns are very much part of my story and always have been. I am a clown partly because of my father's early promptings but also much more because of the promptings of the Holy Spirit – both my earthly and my heavenly fathers are largely to blame! So what are the origins of my faith?

We never really went to church as children. I went to a Methodist church Sunday School three times, got three Bible stickers, and never went again. We were christened in a Methodist church and both my sets of godparents promptly emigrated – they say it was pure coincidence! My grandfather, of whom I am inordinately proud, was a Methodist minister but was more famously a children's broadcaster. He was Romany of the BBC who used to do Children's Hour on the wireless in the 1930s and 1940s. Listeners went 'Out with Romany' on a nature trail and it sounded as though you really were out in the highways and byways. It was all done in the studio, however, and Romany transformed broadcasting in the process. It is odd that, in a sense, I have followed him in resigning from regular ministry at a given church to entertain a much wider populace centred on children and yet just as appropriate for adults. Sadly, my grandfather died in his fifties, ten years before I was born, and I never met him. I guess his family were not too impressed with God at such a turn of events and never really set foot in church again.

I was the last of the triplets to get involved in church and am the only one who still is. Jennie got involved with the local Methodist church in Barnes for a while but it didn't last long. Then Toby started going to our school Christian Union. We were at St Paul's School in London, and the Christian Union was run by old boys from the school. He couldn't, however, persuade me to come – I was a devotee of the Big Match on ITV which was on Sunday afternoons in those days and thus clashed with the Christian Union. I remained deaf to all entreaties, as I still harboured long-held ambitions to be a footballer for Chelsea and England – you can tell what a fool I am! I was nowhere near good enough.

Then the following summer the planned football tour to Germany was called off so I decided I would go to the Christian Union summer house party since all my football playing mates were going to it already. After ten days of football and a strange game called podex, interlaced with prayer times and services, I climbed wearily on to the bus to come home, and burst into tears. I didn't want to leave that halcyon place. Ashfold School in Buckinghamshire encapsulates some of my most cherished memories for it was there that I took my first faltering footsteps of faith. I suddenly realized that there was far more to it than I had thought, and that from starting off just saying prayers, I had actually started to pray. Each morning and evening there were quiet times and I began, when everyone knelt by their bedsides in the dormitory, by simply reciting the Lord's Prayer. But I had moved on and have continued to move on, I hope, though the Lord's Prayer remains a staple diet. And tears have also remained an indispensable part of my faith, life and prayers – but more of that later, too.

At that first summer house party I was fifteen years old. It had been both fun and holy and thus profound. It finished on a Thursday, and the next Sunday I went to what I thought was my parish church: St Mary's in Barnes, near the pond. The service was neither fun nor very holy, I'm afraid. From what little I remember it was bewildering and dull. The vicar, Basil Whitworth, stood menacingly at the door, making sure that none could escape without greeting him and telling him what a lovely service it was (why do clergy do that?!), so I shook him cheerily by the hand. He obviously recognized a stranger in the camp for he asked me first my name and then where I lived. He immediately retorted that this wasn't my parish church at all, that I lived in the parish of St Michael & All Angels, and that I should be going there. He pointed rather severely down the road and I trailed home. What a welcome to the life of the Church! Looking back, perhaps I should have shaken him by the throat.

Undeterred, the following week found me at St Michael's with a friend – much better than risking a solo visit – and that's where I stayed until my ordination. St Michael's was fun and holy too, though in a different way. A hugely high church with yards of lace, bells and smells, it taught me all about theatre and presentation and ritual. I soon became a server and joined in, and it was then that I discovered that while it all had to be done well, it also had to be done rather tongue-in-cheek. It was an early lesson in not letting religion get in the way of faith by not taking it too seriously. Religion is the way you happen to do it, faith is to do with your relationship with God. It's far too easy to worship the furniture or particular words or even a perfectly executed left turn, but it's no substitute for worshipping God. Choreography is only for show, it's not for real. Good choreography points you further on and further in. The vicar was a larger-than-life character called Father Treadwell whom the Bishop of Southwark, Mervyn Stockwood, affectionately referred to as the Pope of Barnes. We were renowned for being 'pre-Vatican 1'! He was, of course, delighted when I went to tell him that I was thinking of being ordained.

I had been on another summer house party, my last before leaving school, though I was to continue to help run the meetings, as we called them, and the house parties for many years yet. Aged seventeen, I was in the process of trying to decide about university and wanted to try to study theology at Oxford. The house party was preceded by a two-day retreat, and during that weekend Eric Hayward, a saint of a man and founder of that school Christian Union, suggested that God might be calling one of us to be ordained and that we shouldn't dismiss the notion. Well, fool that I am, I thought he was talking to me and promptly realized that I wanted to be ordained. I couldn't tell you why – I just knew that I was called. I had no idea what it might involve and that was probably just as well!

I told my mother soon afterwards, with some trepidation, but she was instantly and totally supportive, saying that she knew that I would go in this direction. So it was that I went to Father Treadwell and became the first of his 'boys' – a succession of us from the Christian Union and St Michael's – who ended up being ordained. I never made it to Oxford – they couldn't believe that a long-haired, beer-swilling, football-playing lout really wanted to do theology, never mind be ordained – and I ended up at Bristol University. I had a great time. I can't, however, remember much about the theology. It was all new to me, of course. The exams were pre-set so you got the questions sometimes months before, so there was no pressure for revision. The workload was light, so there was lots of space just to develop and grow, which is surely what education is supposed to help you to do. I came equal bottom in philosophy, though I did pass the exam in the end. I completely gave up on Buddhism. It wasn't the subject that was the problem, it was the young American lecturer with a slow Texan drawl that made the lectures insufferable. We'd been told we could fail one subject, so that's exactly what I did

– I left the exam early and went to the pub! I did an award-winning seminar on the importance of Winnie the Pooh, in the Contemporary Religious Behaviour course, together with great friend Wendy – the other equal bottom in philosophy. I managed to come top in New Testament Greek, largely because you had to translate from Greek into English, and if you recognized any of the passage in question you could just put it in pidgin English and get top marks. As you can tell, I didn't really learn terribly much at Bristol. Theology there was an academic subject that didn't impinge much on my faith or even my own beliefs. It wasn't until I got to Cuddesdon that I had to work out for myself what I actually did believe.

I had been accepted to go forward to training, much to the surprise of the Director of Ordinands. He'd been sure they would tell me to come back in two years and try again. I'm sure I wouldn't be accepted now at all. I didn't fit the bill then and I certainly don't fit any stereotype now. I think the Anglican Church plays too safe these days on the whole, and avoids selecting individuals or taking risks. It was less true in those days. Early on in the selection process I had been sent for interview to a Bishop's Examining Chaplain, who had dismissed my suitability out of hand. His report apparently began: 'This man's spirituality is as scruffy as his appearance . . .'! The Director of Ordinands promised me he would show me the report once I'd been ordained five years, but sadly he died before that was possible. Anyway, I ended up at Ripon College, Cuddesdon – or Colditz, as it was less than affectionately nicknamed.

The less said about my time at Cuddesdon the better, but it was there that the Clown suddenly reappeared. In your final year you had to preach a sermon to the college at the main Friday evening Eucharist. Having a surname Bain, I was billed for the second week – why are things

8

always done alphabetically?! I wasn't worried about preaching – I had done quite a lot of it at the Christian Union meetings and quite enjoyed it. I remember preaching on the God of Tears at one Easter House Party which proved to be rather seminal in my developing thoughts and theology. For the college sermon I admit I didn't want to be boring and to preach on the mundane. As I sat in my room wondering what on earth I could do, it suddenly came to me that I should preach on the idea and image of Jesus as a clown.

In retrospect I would say that was divine inspiration but at the time I was less sure. It came as a complete bolt out of the blue – not an idea I'd thought up at all. Nevertheless, the idea of Jesus as a clown just clicked, and has continued to click ever since. I made myself a red nose out of a sawn-off table tennis ball, painted it red with one of those little pots of enamel for painting model aeroplanes, and fitted some rough and ready elastic to it – I still have that nose in my drawer at home. At an early stage in the sermon I put it on and got a cheap laugh – that's what you're taught, isn't it?! But then I asked the people in the congregation to imagine themselves with a red nose on. I guess quite a few of them would have found that very difficult – it was said in those days that you had to go to Cuddesdon to be a bishop, and there were quite a few students there who definitely seemed to think they were bishop material if not half-way to being bishops already! This was also before the advent of Red Nose Day in the UK, when donning a red nose has become rather more widespread. I then asked them to imagine putting a red nose on the people sitting next to them. That brought gleeful laughter from some as they looked wildly at their neighbours, while others sat resolutely facing forwards but smirking at the thought of it. It's much easier to make a fool of someone else than it is to make a fool of yourself, and clowns should only be found guilty of the latter. It is precisely by making a fool of yourself that others can see how foolish they are – it takes a fool for others to see how foolish they have become. And lastly I asked them to imagine putting a red nose on their image of Jesus. Now some would have found that enormously difficult if not offensive, I suppose, but I then made three points – I'm nothing if not traditional!

Firstly, I think there is lots of humour in the Bible, especially in the pages of the New Testament. Any picture of Jesus worth its salt has to take into account the image of the Jesus who is accused of being a drunkard and the friend of sinners, and work out why this reference is retained in holy writ. We have a Jesus who is expressly contrasted with the dour and itchy John the Baptist as an all-singing, all-dancing pied piper. Jesus's followers are a motley lot of also-rans and ne'er-do-wells, but that is the company he keeps, and it sounds as though it was great fun to sit at his table as well as at his feet. Here was the great raconteur, the jester who spoke the truth, who brought down the mighty from their seats.

Secondly, we have to accept that faith is absurd. It's absurd to believe that God should be born at all, never mind in a two-bit mucky stable in Bethlehem. If I'd been God, I'd have been born in Rome in the equivalent of the Portland Hospital or a five-star hotel – that's where the power was. It's ridiculous to believe that a man should rise from the dead. Why should we? It's not something that happens except in horror films. And yet the fact that it's absurd in the world's eyes doesn't stop it being true, and it is the jester who steps forward to reassure us that he knows that Christ is alive, because he talked to him this morning. If we could only embrace the absurdity of faith and acknowledge the foolishness of God, then we'd be free to do and be what God wants us to be and do.

And thirdly, clowning is about comedy and tragedy, death and resurrection, laughter and tears. You can't have one without the other, and that is why clown humour is so profound. You never know which way it's going to go.

That was the sermon, embellished a bit with the passing of time, I admit. I went and hid in a corner, as I'm prone to, but it was extraordinarily well received. Even now as I travel round the country more than twenty years later, there are people who come up and say they remember that sermon!

Brian Smith, then doctrine tutor, now Bishop of Edinburgh, encouraged me to make it into a thesis. That had to be ten thousand words – more words make it more acceptable I suppose! – and that got an alpha. In doing research for it I discovered kindred spirits, and it was encouraging to know that I wasn't the only person in the world thinking along these lines. Not that it would have mattered because I knew it made sense!

I was duly ordained in Southwark Cathedral. I was made deacon in 1978. There were about twenty of us in three rows and I happened to be on the right-hand end of the front row and thus 'done' first. I had to hold up my service sheet with my name in large bold letters on the back of it so that the short-sighted Bishop of Southwark, Mervyn Stockwood, could know what name to call me. I had Roly on mine. He took one look at it and muttered in a great stage whisper out of the corner of his mouth, 'Is that your baptismal name?' Well, it isn't actually! My real name is Roualeyn – I'm named after a distant ancestor who was a great lion-hunter. But I wasn't going to start spelling that for him so I somewhat nervously said, 'Yes!' There were neither thunderbolts nor earthquakes and all was well. The following year when I was ordained priest he didn't even ask. I've always been called Roly. Kids often ask me as clown what my real name is. I always tell them Roly and they never believe me – at least Bishop Mervyn did! I'm proud of the name Roualeyn and have saddled one of my sons with it as a second name, but to have been ordained Roualeyn wouldn't actually have made sense. If I am called to be a priest I surely come as myself – and that's Roly. He didn't call Roualeyn. I have kept Roly as my clown name partly because it seemed the obvious thing to do, but also because I have always seen my clowning as my vocation and ministry, and to have been ordained Roly is a sign in retrospect of the integrity of that calling and ministry.

I disappeared off to Catford in south-east London to serve as curate in the parish of St George, Perry Hill. The church has now been razed to the ground but that is a coincidence! I wondered if all this clowning malarkey would actually hold water in the real world, but it continued to make even more sense. Increasingly I used stories in my preaching – classic fables, fairy stories, myths, children's stories, but I never dared make any up in those days. Now I'm as much a storyteller as a clown, but story was always at the heart of my proclamation. I started to meet up with others on the same journey. The first was Patrick Forbes, another vicar who was interested in clowning. I read in one of the national papers that he was off to the USA for a clown workshop – and it was news for a vicar to do that sort of thing! I determined that we must meet, and meet we did. After that there was no turning back!

We got a team together to run a huge workshop based on the American model, with an estimated three hundred people coming from the USA for it, and we hoped that at least a hundred would come from this side of the pond.

In the event the Americans pulled out at a late stage and we had a much smaller workshop based at a central London church. In those days we were 'CMPDS', which stood for Clowning, Mime, Puppetry, Dance and Storytelling (in brackets 'in ministry and worship'), and we had teachers for each of those disciplines. Sixty people came, and all were involved in the Sunday morning service. It was quite wonderful. A bishop in the congregation, travelling incognito, said afterwards that it was the most reverent service he had ever been to. It was the first time I put on greasepaint, but apart from a bit of trouble with a stumble and losing my papers trying to get to the pulpit, it was a straight sermon, not unlike my college one. Only a handful of times since have I ever preached straight when in clown dress, and that was at the insistence of the clergy of those churches, because I think that a clown should preach only as a clown would and could – and that isn't in a way that anyone else would or could! Nevertheless we were up and running, and I was suddenly the figurehead of this clown ministry movement. Before long it worked out that it was the clowns doing everything – they still told stories and did all sorts of things but it was the clowns and mimes that featured. We changed our name from the hopelessly unwieldy and totally unrememberable CMPDS (with brackets) to 'Holy Fools', and that loose-knit network and organization has continued ever since in its gentle meandering way. We're rather like the medieval fools and wayside minstrels who found that gentle meandering was the only way and speed to travel. Fools don't move in straight lines when there's a chance of a scenic route and all its concomitant distractions, and nor should they move too quickly in case they miss anything. Every moment has its possibilities, and in this driven, helter-skelter world the fool has much to teach us.

That first workshop was in 1983. By then I was the succentor at Southwark Cathedral. Succentor means sub-cantor, second singer, but I am no singer. I was appointed to work in the community, to be around the place really, though I did have to sing the service occasionally. I hated singing and had no confidence in my ability to hit the right notes – the organist and choirmaster was of a similar opinion! I was a glorified office boy really, the exalted and reverend chair-mover and dogsbody. But there was a team of us and I was far from indispensable. I enjoyed my time there enormously but they were rather obsessed by status and I was right at the bottom of the perceived hierarchy. The fool's job is to bring down the mighty from their seats, and I learnt much about status at the Cathedral. Being essentially a Monday to Friday, nine till five office job, it did give me more time and flexibility for my clowning, and for that I was grateful. It was also at Southwark that I met Jane. Six weeks after our first date I proposed, and three months later we were married at the Cathedral. It was a huge wedding – the Royal Wedding Mark Two, it was nicknamed. The bellringers rang a four-hour peal in the morning, the organist was the same as at the real Royal Wedding of Charles and Diana, the choir sang, clowns acted as ushers, two bishops presided, about seven hundred came. What a day! But the most important thing was that I had discovered real love – I thought I knew what love was before then but it was nothing in comparison. I'd preached about it often enough! I know that I could and would never have done a fraction of what I have done without Jane's encouragement, inspiration and support.

We soon moved to Tooting in south London as I became Vicar of St Paul's, Furzedown. I remained there for six years. We had regular Sunday evening clown workshops for a couple of years, held Clown Advent Carol Services, gave clowns knitted at the local old people's centre to every child baptized, and even hosted the annual Clowns International service for two years, when the clowns' church in Dalston was damaged by fire, so clowning was very much a feature of my ministry. I did an awful lot of the organizing of Holy Fools events, but I was getting frustrated both because I wanted to do more clowning myself and because I needed to take it further. Being the vicar of a parish was restricting both those things. I tried to get a job that would give me more Sundays off – difficult when you're a clergyman! I was shortlisted for an Oxford College chaplaincy and again failed to get to Oxford. I was shortlisted for an ACCM selector, the body that chooses future clergy – that would have been fun if danger-ous! In the end Jane asked me what I really wanted to do and I surprised myself more than her by saying that I wanted to go to Fool Time, which was then the name of the circus school in Bristol, and do their year's course. This really was mad. Our two children, Jack and Sam, were less than three years old, we were living in a tied house in London surrounded by family and friends, and we had no money. But with her encouragement next morning I rang them up. It was Thursday and they said the last auditions were on the following Monday and Tuesday. I went, and much to my delight was offered a place. I'd decided that if they didn't offer me a place I'd go off and be a vicar somewhere else instead, which was a very basic way of putting vocation to the test – if this is right, Lord, then let it happen. . . .

Well, happen it did! Everything fell neatly into place. I resigned from my parish, Jane went back to work as a nurse full-time, Mum paid for an au pair, we found a place to live in Bristol that was ideal – we ended up living in North Street in Bedminster for seven years. And the course was a revelation. I discovered I had a body for a start. Most adults only operate from the neck up – it's certainly true of clergy! – but I discovered that I could communicate with all of me rather than a little part of me. I'd never done acrobatics in my life, apart from a tiny bit at school when I was about eleven. By the end of the year I'd promised myself that I would walk across the stage on my hands – and during the warm-up of the end of the year show I managed it, though I've never tried again since! I learnt to walk on a slackrope, and that continues to be the thing that I enjoy most but also what others enjoy most as I venture in performance on to my Slackrope of Faith. I tried all sorts of things – it was a great time of experimenting. Fool Time gave me the space and time and the where-withal not just to discover much more of the fool inside me but also to give me the confidence to go for it and to do it solo. Before then I knew that I was funny and that I enjoyed clowning, but I'd only ever performed in groups doing skits and stories. Fool Time achieved for me what I'd hoped it would – it took me on to a different level, into a new dimension.

By the end of that year I knew that I wanted to see if I could be a clown full-time. There were doubters of course – many that said it couldn't be done and that it hadn't been done and how could I be sure – but there was plenty of support too. In true fool fashion, we went for it and have never regretted it for a moment. I just said 'yes' to everything! Can you lead a workshop? Yes, I said, though I'd never tried before. Can you do a half-hour show? Yes, though I'd never tried before. I remember well in that first year being rung up by Derby Diocese. They wanted me to lead a day for those clergy in the Diocese who were in the first three years of their ministry. Of course, I said, with huge amounts of trepidation. When asked about my cost for a day I quoted him a price, but he retorted that it wasn't enough and bumped me up to almost double the figure! When he rang again three years later to organize a similar day, he commented that my pricing and bartering skills had obviously improved dramatically!

This was the great learning process. I had come out of Fool Time streets better as a clown and as a performer. I had got rid of my huge red wig and exaggerated make-up in the process. I now had the confidence to do things in my own style. But there's no substitute for actually doing it. You can't be a fool in private – you have to make a fool of yourself in public. And the more that I did, the more I found was possible. The further I went, the fewer the boundaries and restrictions I found. Whereas in the past I had clowned maybe five times in a year, before long I was clowning five times in a week. It began to make an enormous difference. Clowning has a lot to do with pushing and resetting the boundaries, with risking offence in order to achieve that, and with stepping over the precipices if only to discover they are not precipices at all, merely steps and stages on the way to new places.

The pages that follow chart some of that progress and pilgrimage. In 1992 I was asked by HarperCollins to write *Fools Rush In* and I gladly did so. This book covers some of the same ground but it also attempts to include a lot of the stories and events that have marked the years that have passed since then. This includes the practice that, I'm glad to say, has proved the theory correct. But it also takes us further, just as the last eight years have taken me further. It never fails to amaze me how things have developed over those years. Producing books and videos are part of that development. I've travelled all round the world performing and teaching clown ministry. Since that first year I have remained ridiculously busy – or should that be, busy being ridiculous?! If anyone had told me as a would-be full-time clown minister, fresh out of Fool Time, a fraction of the things that have happened, I would never have believed them. Indeed, I might have fled back to a parish in utter panic. But that is true of all of my story.

I was never a performer as a child. I wanted to get into the school plays and always auditioned but the nearest I got to a part was as Banquo's son in Shakespeare's *Macbeth*, and I think that was only because my elder brother Simon was playing Banquo. I had one line. Other than that, my brother Toby and I shared doing the eight ghostly kings in a spoof *Macbeth*. I am not the extrovert of the family – Toby is. I was always rather quiet and infinitely responsible as a teenager – at least that's how I see myself when I look back. I was a safe and solid pair of hands. Toby used mockingly to refer to me as Sunshine. I have always been rather a shy and private person really. There is an expectation from some people when I turn up at a church or some function that, although I'm not in costume and thus not in character, I will be brash, bright and cheerful, frightfully jolly and a laugh a minute. That's definitely not me. I'm quiet and sensible on the whole! And yet, as I hope these pages have already shown, I am also quite different from that. I have tried in this chapter to chart some of the influences that have led me to where I am now. I am an individual who has always dared to try and do what seemed right and not be governed entirely by dull custom, tradition or opinion. I have always tried to pursue my vocation. There are times I have been reckless and ridiculous, other times when I have been too cautious and conservative. But I regret none of it as I head towards the next precipice – there's still no turning back. Ask Lot's wife why not!

I continue to fulfil my childhood ambition in ways that

neither the eight-year-old nor even the thirty-eight-year-old me could ever have dreamt of. The greatest discovery is learning how to play. St Paul's wonderful exaltation of love in his first letter to the Corinthians, chapter thirteen, is a model for all people, never mind Christians, and it is the clown's credo too. I have to admit I'm with St Paul in that when I was a child, I spoke like a child, I thought like a child, I reasoned like a child. But unlike Paul, I've discovered that now I am an adult, I don't have to give up childish things; I don't have to operate solely from the neck up and only within politically and socially correct boundaries; I don't have to be a grown-up all the time. 'Let us play' is the clown's childlike challenge and proclamation. The invitation from Jesus is to become like children or we will never enter the Kingdom of God. Clowns definitely aren't just for children, but they do have to be foolish enough to be like them, for in doing that we become not just heralds and harbingers but signs of that Kingdom: joyful and living sacraments of the living, laughing God. Now that definitely wasn't in my school exercise book, so let's look at the clown more closely.

2

The Calling of Clowns

Every clown in the world is uniquely different – or should be. Just as every person in the world has a distinctive face, so every clown in the world has a different and unique appearance. Toby, my triplet brother, and I look alike and are still often mistaken for each other, but we're quite different really, and those who know us can readily tell us apart. When you see clowns you might think they all look the same really, but they aren't – they are all quite distinct. There is a lovely tradition which Clowns International have re-established of painting a clown's face on an egg. It acts as a kind of copyright, so that no one else can use this face! The faces used to be painted on real blown eggs but those got broken and now china ones are used. They sit on little holders that represent the clown's personal costume. So mine has his dog collar, check suit and a Canterbury cap. The collection is housed in the Clowns' Gallery in Hackney in east London.

Part of the reason for the difference in every clown face is the fact that the design of a clown's face is totally dependent on the real face that's underneath. Greasepaint only accentuates and exaggerates what's there and so should be an aid to communication. It's not there to look pretty. The clown with a big red smile plastered over his mouth can only smile – he or she can't register any other emotions. The greasepaint should help the face work, not limit its expressions. Even if one were to try to copy another clown's face, it is unlikely to end up the same. One year when I was teaching clown ministry at Clown Camp in the USA, the director, Richard Snowberg, got ten of the staff to put their own clown face on one of the other staff members. I had to swap clown faces with Brenda Marshall, a lovely American whiteface clown from Texas who also specializes in clown ministry. My face is very simple: a bit of red on the lips with a circle at each end, a red painted nose, rouge on the cheeks, a simple cross on each cheek done with eyeliner, and eyeliner under the eyes. But it looked quite different on Brenda. She has much higher cheekbones and a different shaped face – I had to make the crosses much shorter, the circles much smaller. We both have short dark hair so that was OK, but we were different. Then she put her face on mine: a complete white base and a much prettier, sparkly design, and a wig. I looked much more like her than she did me! That is largely because of the white base which obliterates what's beneath. I've seen people do a whole clown ministry routine based on putting on greasepaint, where we start with a clean sheet, a blank page on which God can start to work, and then the colours get added, each representing different things. Anyway, I still could never have passed myself off as Flower, which is her clown name.

You're also not supposed to use a name that any other clown has. Having said that, there are about seven thousand Rainbow the Clowns in the world, most of them in the USA, nearly all of them sporting gaudy rainbow wigs! You can pass down a name and even a face from one generation to another. My early hero Coco's son is Coco in America, while Charlie Cairoli's son and Emmett Kelly's son are both named the same as their fathers. But, of course, if I ask a bunch of children to draw a clown and then think of a name to give their clown, a lot of them end up as Roly the Clown. If we paint their faces, they want to be like me – very flattering, I know! What remains fairly extraordinary is how synonymous Coco's name became with clowning. Even now if I walk down the street in clown, often as not someone will shout out 'Hello Coco!' or something similar. He lies buried in Woodnewton near Peterborough, and one summer, when Clowns International had helped raise money to build a village hall in his memory, we gathered around his gravestone for a service, which I led rather nervously. Very moving.

Names are important. There are all sorts of ways of choosing a clown name but the best way is to find it out for yourself. You know when you've got the right name. Some clowns have used that second name given them by their parents which they've always found embarrassing, or that childhood nickname that was even worse; others have a play on words of their usual name; some choose a name that's just silly; others choose a fruit or vegetable or other foodstuff – Strawberry is popular, as is Pickle, and there's a Rhubarb too. I wonder if there's a Cucumber somewhere – it sounds quite good if you want to be a cool clown! Clowns with Ringling Bros in the USA just use their real name, Christian name and surname, which does seem a bit odd. Since the clown is an extraordinary character it seems sensible to be called by an extraordinary name. Roly is my own name, but it's sufficiently unusual for it to work. There are plenty of names for plenty of reasons, and as long as the name fits, that's fine.

The fact that every clown is different makes it impossible to define the clown – the clown would probably roll around the floor in hysterical mirth if I even attempted it. Yet there are types of clown and these are much simpler to distinguish. In circus there are three – four if you include character clowns who are, as the name suggests, individual characters. The major type of clown, and the one that most people conjure up in their mind's eye when you mention clowns, is the auguste. Coco was an auguste. He is the clumsy idiot, clothed in ill-fitting attire in which everything is too tight or too baggy and certainly utterly tasteless. Shod in enormous boots, he is forever putting his great big foot in it and taking trips and tumbles. Auguste gets everything hopelessly wrong and yet gloriously right. He's the one who gets the custard pies in the face and is routinely drenched with buckets of water. He's the one who never sees it coming. But he has a great time. He gets all the love, all the laughter and all the sympathy. He takes us with him into his own world and we're drawn by his magic and dragged along by his logic. In his world all things are possible, for it is a world of hopes and dreams brimful with possibilities.

I'm basically an auguste. At a church in Wantage there was a man with an enormous beard sitting rather curled up in the pew behind several rows of children over to my left, and he looked a little out of place. He had a twinkle in his eye and I could see he was enjoying the service. Afterwards he came up and thanked me, saying, 'You brought us all into your own world. It was extraordinary. Thank you. It was marvellous.' But that's what Auguste does – he brings us out of the ordinary into the extraordinary, and with his transforming touch, all things and all places are changed. Lou Jacobs, the famous American clown, was a classic auguste – his face appeared on American stamps before he died. A tall man, he added a bit extra to the top of his head and topped it with a tiny hat to make it look even longer and himself even bigger. With exaggerated features and a big red nose, he was larger than life, yet he was also a contortionist and he used to wrap himself inside a tiny car to drive into the ring, and then out would come this enormous clown. One of his classic props was a motorized bath in which he used to race round the ringside whilst scrubbing his back and spurting water. Auguste is full of surprises and brings absolute bedlam. Slapstick is his trade and medium, and mess is what he revels in. The Rastellis do a marvellous sequence of prop-based gags. One of them gets his head knocked off and then the trunk of his body is lifted off too – and off scuttles the clown ducked down inside. On comes a grand piano which one of them starts to play, so another brings on a cannon, aims it at the piano and fires, the piano explodes and a huge shell is seen to be stuck through our pianist, who wildly tries to pull it out! Madness! But Auguste is this kind of indestructible cartoon character who survives all manner of assault and battery and comes up smiling, asking for more – and we love him all the more for doing so. Mischievous and playful, he just loves to play the fool and, despite all his excesses, he is always and utterly forgiven and forgivable. He is ourselves writ large.

But alongside him in circus is Whiteface, and he's another kettle of fish entirely. Kettle is quite a good description of him actually – he's bright and shiny, and Auguste just brings him to the boil till steam pours out of his ears! Whereas Auguste appears to be the happy misfit, Whiteface is elegance personified. Whereas Auguste seems to have very little control over anything, least of all himself, Whiteface is very definitely in charge – or at least he thinks he is! Traditionally, Whiteface is dressed in sequins, with unblemished white stockings and stylish white shoes. He or she is likely to have a whole wardrobe of costumes that outdo each other in sparkling *elan*. A little white felt conical hat tops his white face, and on the white face are his distinctive markings: a little red on the lips and under the nostrils so that the audience can delineate his basic features, red ears by tradition, eyeliner to make his eyes work, and then his eyebrows – those are what distinguish him from all the others. Whereas each auguste has a completely different face, Whiteface has a different eyebrow or eyebrows. The sweep and curl of the eyebrows tell you which whiteface you're watching! There are very few English whitefaces now, though there are plenty in clown troupes in Europe. All through the 1990s Alexis was the superb whiteface at Zippo's Circus, with Tweedy as the wonderfully anarchic auguste. Alexis was definitely in charge of proceedings in his ringmaster type role, but Tweedy was never far away, loitering with playful intent.

Whiteface is clever, though not as clever as he thinks he is. He has a proper musical instrument which he plays with style and dignity. Auguste is likely to play the most unlikely invention of an instrument and have much more fun. Whiteface is impossibly pompous, though there remains a twinkle in his eye – after all, he is part of the fun and knows it really. But Auguste is there to bring down the mighty from their seats, and bring Whiteface down he does, every time. It's the old double act with straight man and funny man: Ernie Wise as Whiteface to Eric Morecambe's Auguste, or Dean Martin to Jerry Lewis, Stan Laurel to Oliver Hardy. The trouble with Whiteface is that he takes himself too seriously, and the trouble with people who take themselves too seriously is that they can't be taken seriously at all – it's just that people who take themselves too seriously don't realize it! Whiteface is more than happy to boss Auguste around and treat him like a servant. Auguste is the servant clown, dare we suggest at this early stage, the suffering servant, and Auguste will always do what he's told, or at least attempt to. All sorts of things happen to him, but Auguste is irrepressible. Down he goes and back he bounces, bouncing back to do his duty and bouncing off Whiteface himself, the source and butt of so much of his tomfoolery. Whiteface continues to get both more apoplectic with Auguste and more apologetic to the audience about Auguste for being such a disgrace, but in the end it is Auguste who comes out on top and everybody cheers. Whiteface is the original clown and still yearns to retain or regain his pre-eminence, but Auguste usurps his role time and again.

Auguste was created by accident, which is highly appropriate for such an accident prone character. The story goes that an acrobat called Tom Belling was working for Ernest Renz's circus in the 1864 season in Berlin. He had been suspended for four weeks as a punishment for falling during his act, but he'd crept into the circus, stuck a wig on his head back-to-front and put a coat on inside-out, to amuse himself as much as his colleagues. Suddenly Renz appeared, and Belling in his haste to escape simply backed away at great speed but straight into the ring, where he fell head over heels in a heap. The audience screamed with delight, assuming it to be part of the act. Like all good circus-goers brought up to interact with the performers, they shouted, 'August! August!', which was the traditional German nickname for a clumsy idiot, and so a new clown was born and christened all in one go. It is ironic that Whiteface, who always tries to be so august and seem so splendid, should have such a contrasting sidekick as the less than august Auguste.

But if Whiteface thinks that Auguste is unworthy of him, then what must he think of Tramp? Whiteface in all his glad rags has to cope with Tramp, clad in real rags. Tramp is the first proper sad clown. A po-faced, slow-paced loner, he doesn't seem to want to join in with all the others, and yet, of course, he does really. He looks terribly battered, yet there is a twinkle in his eye. He elicits endless sympathy but rarely cracks a smile. When he does it's worth waiting for. He's always on the edge of things, on the outside looking in. He's often on the edge of doing something, and yet he never quite gets there. Otto Griebling, perhaps the best tramp clown there has ever been, used to do a running gag where he was trying to deliver a parcel to a named and of course fictitious member of the audience. Each time he brought it in, it got more and more dilapidated till it was obviously beyond repair, and off he'd go again, quite forlorn, and you knew he'd keep on looking. Emmett Kelly, the other great tramp clown, used to have terrible trouble trying to crack a peanut with his teeth. In the end he'd go off and come back with an enormous sledgehammer which he slammed down on the peanut, leaving it, of course, crushed into dust and totally inedible. Off he'd go again, baleful and slump-shouldered, in search of another meal.

Otto Griebling and Emmett Kelly both originated in American circus, though Emmett Kelly became very popular over here when he joined Bertram Mills in England for several seasons. In America they had and still have three-ring circuses, even five-ring circuses sometimes, with acts going on simultaneously in all of them. Tramp originated partly because of the fact that most of the clown gags and entrees had therefore to be big and visual, with sometimes fifteen to twenty clowns taking part. You couldn't have a solo clown doing his thing in one of the rings. So suddenly Tramp appeared, stubbled and stumbling, up in the bleachers, round the edges, rarely in the middle, and, of course, alone. Emmett Kelly used to have a rancid old cabbage that he'd nibble at and then offer wistfully to someone in the audience. It was individual one-to-one clowning that offset the big set-piece stuff beautifully.

Legend also has it that Tramp also arose in response to what was happening in the States at the time, namely the Great Depression. There is no doubt that the scruffy hobo was a familiar sight around America, so perhaps Tramp's popularity can be ascribed to the fact that here was a sympathetic character down on his luck that most could identify with and be grateful that 'There but for the grace of God go I'. It certainly helped Emmett Kelly, but there seem to have been tramp clowns before him in circus, as there certainly were in film. Charlie Chaplin springs jauntily to mind. W. C. Fields started off as a tramp juggler in vaudeville before moving into films. But it's a nice thought that Tramp maybe went to the circus looking for a job, and that as we watch him, he's actually still looking . . .

There's a lot of Tramp in me. The divisions between types are far from hard and fast. People often say or shout to me, 'Smile, you're a clown!', as I sit quietly in a corner or stand puzzled by a pulpit. But what Tramp teaches us is that you don't have to be happy, smiling, funny people all the time in order to make people laugh. That's one-dimensional. Nor do you have to be huge and outrageous, though there is the need for simplification and exaggeration. If you're a solo clown, Tramp is an obvious clown to be, and my clown plays with failure endlessly, if only to show that failure isn't the ogre that society has caricatured it to be. It can be rather fun really! An awful lot of comedy, certainly in clowning, is based on or derives from failure. One of my constant punchlines is, 'If at first you don't succeed, smile: God loves a cheerful failure.' Tramp remains far too solemn to be a cheerful failure, but still we laugh as he resolutely but perversely perseveres against all odds in the midst of predicaments that are somehow only too familiar to us all. It is perhaps this happy hopelessness that actually gives us hope as we realize that nothing is as good or as bad as it seems. It has been said of my clowning that it is always hoping against hope, and in the end we see and rejoice in the triumph of hope over experience. Perhaps the best clowns never learn from experience, they just hope. Whiteface would, of course, disagree wholeheartedly with that because he relies on being sensible and has learnt from his mistakes – not that he's ever made any, you understand! But clowns have become symbols of hope in a success-driven world which has begun to realize that success isn't all it's cracked up to be.

Auguste, Tramp and Whiteface are quite distinct characters and they work beautifully together, but it isn't quite as simple as that. In America, for instance, the characters are quite different – or at least Whiteface is. They don't like their clowns to be proud and arrogant, so all their clowns have to 'have a nice day'. This means that a lot of their clowns have a whiteface base with auguste features. It also means they miss out on much of the fun and failure that European clowns have because they don't have the same dynamic and interaction between the pompous and the playful. These basic types originate in circus, but only a small percentage of clowns in the world actually work in circuses. There are clowns who only do children's parties, clowns who do corporate events, clowns who do walkaround commercial jobs; clowns in churches, theatres, prisons, schools, fairs and galas; clowns who teach, clowns who do balloon sculptures, clowns who do magic; clowns who do parades, clowns who do shows, clowns who meet and greet. The list is endless. There are all sorts of clowns in all sorts of places, although circus is where we think they belong. There's a lot to be said for that, and we'll come back to it in the next chapter, but as long as a clown is a clown and not just dressed up as one, he or she is definitely a clown. I have a rule of thumb that says if you can do what you do without a red nose on, then do it without the red nose and wear a different costume.

I think a clown has to be three things: extraordinary, funny and truthful. A clown has to be extraordinary because he or she wants to take us out of the ordinary, out of ourselves to glimpse and even visit that different world that the clown both inhabits and represents. Hence the painted face and outlandish costumes. Hence the expectation that clowns can do magic or walk on ropes or do both silly and strange things, and what they have in their pockets beggars belief. A clown has to be funny because a clown's basic function is to make us laugh. The clown doesn't have to be funny all the time but if there is no laughter then we wonder what on earth is happening – or isn't, as the case may be! The secret of being funny is exactly that: being funny. It is a rare gift – given to more people than we think – to simply be funny. And the funniest clowns are those who are simply funny. Doing funny things can still be very funny for the audience – and that's where we all start! – but actually allowing ourselves to be funny in all our natural absurdity is the beginning of real clowning. Because that is part of the process of being truthful. The best clowns, indeed all clowns, have to be true to themselves because only then can they be the jesters, the truth-tellers, the ones who are licensed to speak the truth. Humour and truth go hand in hand. It's often said that the funniest things are those that happen naturally, they're true to life. And truth can only be conveyed – it can't be spelt out; it can be glimpsed, seen and understood, but it can't be written in capital letters or necessarily researched. We seek truth rather than look it up in the reference section. And humour allows us to get the joke, to have that moment of revelation when suddenly everything makes sense. Truth rings bells, just as the jester's hat used to! So whether, like me, you are involved in clown ministry and want somehow to speak of Truth with that capital 'T', or whether you are happy just to make people laugh, you still have to be truthful and seek your own truth if not the Truth. When clowns seek truth or Truth, extraordinarily funny things happen as well as extraordinary ones . . . !

The connections between clowns and the gods have long been recognized in all sorts of different cultures throughout history. Time and again the clown has been seen to possess powers that other 'ordinary people' don't have. So the village idiot was treated with a certain reverence and compassion that puts today's society to shame. Dwarves have always played the fool as jesters, but they have also often acted as witch doctors and shamans. Clowns in old native American tribes would enact comic exorcisms, and the witch doctor would have the fool's licence to stretch and break boundaries, to establish as well as banish taboos. The clowns were the messengers of the gods who could communicate with both man and the gods and act as their go-between. Shakespeare is the most famous proponent of the wisdom of fools, but he was only putting into print and into the public domain what mankind has always recognized: that the fool has a wisdom to which others can only aspire. The fool has a prophetic role and function, speaking of unpalatable truths in ways that make them digestible, and reminding others of their own folly, not necessarily through either deed or word but in his own person and presence.

I went to the Rochester Diocesan Conference in 1997, which was held down in Bognor at what used to be Butlins, but the Conference could hardly have been described as a holiday camp! I remained in costume and character throughout, and just my being there was highly provocative. We'll come back to some of that later! I ended up doing all sorts of things, as always, but one of the main things had been totally unplanned: I did a kind of double act with the Dean of King's College, London, Richard Burridge, each morning. He was doing the Bible Study but I did a clowning preface each time, and it was great fun. The two of us were then asked to do a kind of resume or reflection on the Conference on the final day, including our impressions of the Diocese. We were the only two 'outsiders' who had been there throughout, which was why we were accorded this dubious privilege. I didn't know what to say but ended up saying an awful lot just by relaying some of the things that happened in those few days, telling the story of my conference, and urging them to be foolish enough to climb out of their entrenched positions and be foolish and faithful without my help in the future. The effect of my few foolish words was quite extraordinary and they somehow defined the Conference for most people present. The words on their own wouldn't have been so conclusive without the four days of clowning that had gone before and all the responses and reactions that that had provoked, but I beg to suggest, from all the feedback I've had in letters as well as the Diocesan newspaper coverage, that Rochester Diocese can never be quite the same again! One report admitted, 'I am feeling grateful for those who decided to invite our holy clown to be with us throughout. They may not have realized the risk they were taking in letting loose upon us Roly's irreverent but prophetic mixture of play and pathos! But the one who seemed at times to be threatening order, was in the end the one who held the event together.' Another reporter suggested, 'One of the best things was a clown – a wonderful man. He upset a lot of people and delighted others – but that's in the ancient tradition of "the fool". Remember your Shakespeare. He had the fool's gift of going to the heart of things, pricking bubbles with satire.' And another concluded that, 'We didn't expect to learn anything new from a clown but I don't think there were many present who left without having been touched profoundly by his presence. Roly was both funny and tragic, subtle and predictable, profound yet simple in his teaching, deeply sincere and showing an awe for God that many of us keep hidden deep within us.' I quote these not to blow my own trumpet and say how wonderful I am, though I think the clown should always be full of wonder, but to try and show the impact that the clown can have in all sorts of ways on all sorts of people. You never really know what's happening at the time and that's the way it should be, but I just try to remain true to my calling, follow my instincts and see what happens next. To achieve that at all you have to remain an outsider. The clown is called to and must remain on the edges – it's where he belongs. It's a lonely place, but however often he leaps into the middle of things with surprising ease and gusto, he must always return to the wilderness, eschewing the comfort zones for the sake of prophecy and truth. It is why the clown can never be 'one of us' for he is always seen as somehow 'other'. And yet the clown is all of us and each of us, mirroring our foibles and presenting dreams and possibilities that we never dared think of and yet recognize as our own. It may be that it is the clown's voice we sometimes hear crying in our wilderness, preparing a way for the Lord.

The somewhat mystic dimension of the clown as prophet can be seen more prosaically in the role of the clown as political commentator. This is particularly true of the old Soviet Union where the clowns of the circus were the real court jesters, self-styled Jesters to Her Majesty the People. It fell to the clowns to say the things that needed saying in a society with no free speech. It didn't always work, of course. In 1907, Durov, a Russian clown performing in circus in Germany, was arrested and charged with treason. He did an act with a pig. Durov would place a German officer's cap or helm in the middle of the ring for the pig to fetch. The pig would bring it back dutifully, but then, thanks to a bit of ventriloquism, would shout 'Ich will helm', meaning 'I want the helmet'. But, of course, it could also mean 'I am Wilhelm', who was the German Emperor, and the Kaiser was not amused. Durov defended his case and was acquitted, which is a classic case of Auguste making sure that Whiteface gets his come-uppance. But in Europe there is a much stronger tradition of overtly political clowning, of clowning with a particular purpose or target, and I suspect it is because it is only ultimately the clown who dares to speak freely in those places where no one else is allowed to. Cartoonists and stand-up comedians fulfil that function in the UK, and the animated puppets of *Spitting Image* take it to the brink, but none of them would get arrested for their comments and antics. It would be terribly unBritish to belie a lack of sense of humour evidenced by arresting someone for having one!

As long as the clown or cartoonist or comedian gets it right and is funny and truthful, you're in no danger. If, however, you get it wrong you're in trouble. Today you might get less work or lose a job, but the old court jesters could pay for it with their lives. Durov was to be banished from Germany but was saved by the law. More often the old court jesters lived and were saved by their wit as much as their wits. So the story is told of Scogin who, having been banished from England by the King and told never to set foot on English soil again, reappeared at the court soon after. Challenged by the King, Scogin smiled mischievously, removed one of his shoes and poured a small pile of earth on to the ground in front of him. 'But sire', he complained, 'I stand on French soil!' He stayed after that. Conversely, Golet, court fool to William of Normandy, was his master's eyes and ears, and managed to warn him of impending assassination, thus saving the future William the Conqueror's life – another fool who changed the course of British history!

The peril of getting involved in political clowning is that you tend to lose your impartiality before you get near losing your head. The clown must surely remain an independent and free spirit, unmastered and unfettered. The King may think he is the Jester's master but he isn't, just as Whiteface is in no way Auguste's master. So, just as the clown was always the messenger and go-between for the gods, representing one to the other, so the clown fulfils that function in other places too. I clowned in a school in the North of England where the chaplain had always seen himself as the school jester, and tried to maintain that role. He was not there as the Headmaster's ventriloquist's dummy, nor was he strictly on the side of the staff, but neither was he there just for the pupils. He always tried to remain in the no-man's-land between and amongst them all, and that can be a place of great anguish, as he found to his cost. He was great fun, a natural clown, classically eccentric and nonconformist, as clowns must be, and he dared to ask questions and say the things he thought needed to be said. He's not there any more but the clown always moves on, and I hope he's remembered that ultimately kings never win!

The clown's task isn't just to amuse, though amuse he must. He's there to ask questions of us. Grock, one of the great clowns of the twentieth century, always asked 'Why?', and it's a question that isn't asked often enough. A child keeps asking why and soon has it drummed out of him or her, and perhaps that's why we don't ask it nearly so much when we're adults – we just think it rather a lot. So the clown takes the child's place and asks the question for us. He's not so worried about who or when or where, just why. And the other side of the coin is that he also asks 'Why not?', which is often far more pertinent and rather more disturbing. 'Because we've always done it like that,' isn't a good enough answer, nor is 'It's never been done before.' The clown takes nobody and nothing for granted, and he always sees everything as if it's for the first time – so it doesn't matter if it is truly the first time, it just adds to the excitement and the possibilities. There's a sense in which the clown doesn't really want to know the answer to his questions at all, especially if they're long-winded and boring and terribly reasonable; he just wants to be sure that the question has been asked, because only then can we move on. No respecter of persons in terms of people's reputations, he takes each person and project and moment on its merits. When the Second Emperor of Qin decided in the third century BC that he would have the Great Wall of China lacquered, it was an extraordinarily mad idea and would have cost a fortune in terms of human lives, never mind finance. But the Emperor was the Emperor and no one could gainsay the madness, apart from the fool, whose name was Twisty Pole. He applauded the idea of making the wall not just beautiful but smooth and shiny and slippery so that enemies couldn't climb up and over it, but he wondered about the simple practicalities of building a big enough drying room . . . In the laughter that ensued, the Emperor suddenly saw the error of his ways, and the preposterous project was swept hastily under the carpet. Had it not been for the fool, it would have happened.

The clown gets to the heart of things. His secret is his

simplicity. KISS is the clown's mnemonic: Keep It Simple, Stupid. Yet the clown isn't simple at all, if by simple we mean stupid. The clown plays the fool. He doesn't need to know what happens next nor even why he's doing what he's doing or saying what he's saying. He concentrates on the simplicity of the now, on the present moment in all its sacredness, and the rest can wait till he gets there. Perhaps in that childlikeness lies the secret of his wisdom, for it is that which gives him the capacity to see and even make all things new. There is a wisdom in *naïveté* that returns us to the gods, and in my experience it is something of this that has brought me and others much closer to God than I or they would otherwise have dreamt of.

'Unless you become like children you will never enter the Kingdom of God,' is a familiar warning from the lips of Jesus, and most of us remain deaf to its entreaty – we'd rather be grown-up and respected as such, thank you very much. Enter the clown, the so-called children's entertainer, stage left, and it's no wonder that some people get worried. But then 'What if . . . ?' must give way to 'Why not?', and when that happens we suddenly see that the clown is not just beckoning us into his world but into the Kingdom – and then who knows what will happen next! The Kingdom is where the clown, the jester, the truth-teller belongs, but it's also the place where we all belong. It's just that it sometimes takes a clown to remind us and point the way. So be careful next time you hear the clown calling – it might just be important . . .

3

Circus and Sacrament

I've already admitted that my father always took me to the circus every Christmas, and that's when I knew that Christmas was calling. But the circus calls lots of people to come and enter its magnificent domain and be dazzled by its spectacle. Many come to watch but some come to watch and then stay – there's a parable of the Kingdom for you! But I don't think circus is just a spectacle. There is something sacramental about circus inasmuch as it can speak of the things of God and be a means of his grace as well as a sign of it. The circus at its best is a mysterious but also a mystical world. Today one of the most popular and spectacular circuses is the French Canadian Cirque du Soleil. They create whole new worlds in each of their shows, with young incredibly gifted and versatile performers in multi-coloured extravagant costumes doing outrageous stunts in perfect unison and harmony, one after the other and yet all amongst each other. This is Circus Theatre at its best really, where circus is part of the telling of the story, part of the creating of the atmosphere, part of sustaining the wonder and never for its own sake. There is always something happening and it doesn't matter if you can't follow the plot. One of the constant themes is the attempt to entice the ordinary passer-by to join in the madness and the revelry and be part of this different and exciting world. This is circus reinvented and it is quite delightful and exhilarating. It doesn't have any animals but it still has its clowns – you can't have circus without clowns. And clowns are the signs and signposts along the way.

Circus as we know it is comparatively new – just over two hundred years old. The first circus was established by a cavalryman called Philip Astley in 1770, on premises where Waterloo Station in London now stands, and then known as Ha'penny Hatch. Astley had started with a roped off area in a field, but in 1769 he acquired the mortgage and then came the first circus building, Astley's Amphitheatre. He was a gifted and skilled horseman and was the main attraction with a series of trickriding and daredevil stunts. He soon realized, however, that a bit of variety was required, and along came the clowns led by one called Burt, and with them came acrobats and slackrope vaulters – and modern circus was born.

So circus started with horses – the ring is the size it is because it is the optimum size for a horse to keep going round in a circle. But it is the clowns who create the atmosphere, the clowns who hold everything together, and the clowns who put everything in perspective. When I lead a children's workshop on clowning or circus skills in the UK, I always ask how many of them have been to the circus. Usually about half of them have. And if I then ask what they enjoyed most, the largest percentage say they enjoyed the clowns most. Now that may be because they've got one standing in front of them, but it's probably a fair reflection of what kids think. In the old days a lot of the clowns would be gymnasts and riders who had been injured at some stage and rather fell into clowning, and many of them made good clowns. But the great clowns are quite different – dare we suggest that many are called but few are chosen?! The clowns can make or break a circus. It is the clowns with their humour who set circus apart.

The clowns form a relationship with their audience in a way that none of the other performers can. Their performance depends on the sustaining of a relationship with each of the members of the audience. The tightrope walker and the juggler and the trapeze artiste and all the other glamorous stars of the circus perform their wondrous deeds, and 'style' occasionally when they want to garner their applause, and that's the limit of their relationship. The clowns need to win you over, make you laugh, elicit your sympathy, keep surprising you, carry on conversations with you, and even, wonder of wonders, invite you into the ring itself. They keep coming back for more – as the ringmaster knows to his cost! By the end of the show the good clown has got friends for life all round the Big Top, friends who will certainly never forget him, and friends who will pick up the traces of that relationship when the circus comes back next year. You can't have that sort of relationship with the ringmaster, who is the figure of authority – it would be like being best friends with the head teacher. But the clown is back to doing his traditional job – he's the go-between between the circus, represented by the ringmaster and all the glamorous gods who fly through the air with the greatest of ease and do miraculous deeds, and us mere mortals. And it is the clown who provides us with the access as well as the wherewithal to be part of it all. It is a very priestly function and one that lies at the heart of a theology of circus as well as of the clown himself.

Sitting on the edges of the spectacular Cirque du Soleil, it is the mischievous playmakers who make the connections with us and beckon us on and in, not the stars in their firmaments. It is the clowns we trust implicitly, in all their madness. Part of the reason for that is because they make us laugh, and we are always grateful for the gift of laughter.

Genuine laughter is a great reminder and sign of the presence of the playful God in mankind. But the clowns also make us laugh at ourselves and at our own responses. They put our sense of admiration and awe in perspective by lampooning the breathtaking acts that have gone before. In biblical terms they bring the Towers of Babel crashing down with no apparent problem at all! In any traditional circus, a troupe of liberty horses all working in perfect time and unison might be followed by the clown on a hobby-horse or a Shetland pony; the strongman's mighty exertions might be followed by the clown in a leopardskin flailing polystyrene weights; the death-defying flying trapeze act are brought down to earth by the clown enjoying the comforts of the safety net as either hammock or trampoline or both. The clown constantly brings down the mighty from their seats so that none of them can take themselves too seriously, none can be too zealously starlike. In the process the clown somehow convinces us that we could do it too – if we dare, and if we practise enough! For these circus performers are really mere mortals too. And that gives us hope and the possibility of grace.

The clown knows that the only thing that limits us is ourselves, so he wants to take us out of ourselves, transcend our horizons, venture forth and come with him. It is no wonder that part of the mythology of circus is that it is the place that people run away to. For a moment we suddenly know that we are infinitely capable of all sorts of things, but most of us let the moment pass, with perhaps just a slight pang of regret. Fortunately there are others who are taken by both the dream and the reality, they grasp the moment and never let go. Yet the circus is also the place that people run away from because it is far too scary, too nonconformist, and it keeps on moving. It is a pilgrim community, and that's a challenge to those of us who like deep roots and a solid status quo! That is silly really, because the circus too is deeply traditional, bound by its rituals and customs, and remains a very close-knit community and fellowship. They live their lives cheek by jowl, and their lives might literally depend on each other. If you risk your life on a daily basis, you have to trust the rest of the community to help you do it and through it. The circus is a good model of living in community, and with its almost monastic disciplines, it's a pretty good model for the Church. Also, with the clowns around, it can't take itself too seriously – but that's another chapter as well as the secret of maintaining health and sanity!

The other very practical function of the clowns is that they are always on hand in times of trouble and emergency. If anything goes wrong in the circus, such as when the trapeze artiste falls to the ground or anyone has an accident or for some reason the next act isn't ready to go, the clowns have to step in to fill and breach the gap. Their traditional changing room is known as Clown Alley, and it is always situated next to the entrance at the back so that at a moment's notice they can leap into the fray and divert, distract and amuse the waiting audience. The clowns are the ones who pick up the pieces, who keep reassuring us that all is well and all shall be well, and we applaud them for their courage in our gratitude for their ministry.

But clowns belong in the circus ring, metaphorically as well as historically, for in the ring there is nowhere to hide. The ring is a magical place but it is also the vulnerable place, and the clown soon discovers both to his cost and to his delight that it is the only place to be, and it keeps drawing him back. It is only when we enter and tarry awhile in the vulnerable places that we begin to fathom not only the constituent parts of which we are made but also the possibilities of what we may be in time to come. The ring is the place where dreams can become reality, and where we can all be transformed if not transfigured. It is a perilous place but also a place of grace and wonder. Clowns are vulnerable lovers and they are the ring's crazed but compassionate commissionaires, who happily fling open the doors for us all to come in. Clowns have to be vulnerable for they need to be open, not just to every person but to every possibility. Every moment has the potential for playfulness, triumph and disaster. Each individual person has her own needs and hopes and dreams. The clown has somehow to be sensitive enough to keep all that in balance, skilful enough never to miss a trick, and funny enough, of course, to make us laugh – through him – at ourselves.

Clowns are lovers because they not only accept all people but would do anything for you, even die for you – as they do, regularly, in the ring. They genuinely care, and they want everyone to be their friends and playmates. I remember taking my two sons, Sam and Jack, to a circus when they were aged about four and six. Two guys who had done their trapeze act earlier suddenly reappeared dressed as clowns, and they started beating people round the head with rolled-up newspapers. Obviously they had been told that it is funny if a clown does that sort of thing. Well, I was terrified, as were the boys. It just wasn't funny. There was no sense of play or love in such manic and macho violence. The essence of slapstick is that it is a parody of violence, not the real thing! And clowns do it to each other or to themselves before they go and find someone else who wants to join in, who wants to come and play too. Clowns need happy playmates not hapless victims, so all the laughter and the jokes must be at the clown's expense and nobody else's.

If a clown races in and throws a bucket of water all over you, you're unlikely to be amused, not least because you've got to sit soaking for the rest of the show. But if a clown is standing drenched in front of you and has reduced you to hysterics in the process, you are far less likely to object if a bit of spray comes your way. Indeed, some of us are grateful because it includes us in the mayhem and grants us a kind of temporary membership of the clown troupe. It's not unlike the church ritual of the asperges, where holy water is sprinkled or sprayed over a congregation. It's a rite that is often used at the Renewal of Baptismal Vows, reminding us of our membership in the Body of Christ and of the vows made at our baptism. When I was a server at St Michael's in Barnes this was a regular practice, especially at Easter, and it always caused barely repressed mirth. Father Treadwell was a mean shot with his holy water brush, and many a member of the congregation would get it in the eye. As acolyte carrying my candle, I would solemnly process down the aisle and move to one side to let the choir through. But then I had to try and keep a straight face as they passed by with hymn books dripping and with strange wet patches on their otherwise dry and spotless choir robes. Now tell me how different that celebration of a sacrament is from the circus with its great high priest, the clown, with his enormous decorator's brush spraying his blessings on the faithful who have gathered there together . . .

The circus has this sacramental, church-like quality. Flags flying and music playing, the Big Top beckons and welcomes us in, friend or stranger. Unmistakably what it is because of its design and architecture, we think we know what to expect but inevitably we hope for the unexpected too: for surprise and revelation as well as awe and laughter. It speaks of a different kingdom which is yet inhabited by mortal men, women and children called to greater things. It is a place of mystery, miracle and truth, where the apparently impossible becomes suddenly possible and we are touched, if not changed, profoundly. Church and circus are both ordinary and extraordinary, human and divine, and if we take the enormous risk of joining in, things will never be quite the same again. The essence of the sacraments of the Church is that they are ordinary things like bread and wine and water that are transformed into extraordinary channels of God's grace. That's what I think the circus can be and do.

Whenever I've taken part in services in Big Tops, it has been quite extraordinary. Usually they have been packed for they are indeed Special Services. There were great practical problems in pitching Zippo's Big Top in the close at Salisbury Cathedral, not least because we had to let the tyres down on the loader lorry which carried the big top canvas in order to get it through the archway into the close. Nevertheless it was worth the effort!

But the most memorable service in a big top that I've been part of was back in 1988, before I even went to circus school. In those days I still had my big red wig and I was still a vicar! It was the end of the Clowns International Convention down in Bognor Regis in Sussex, and that year about five hundred clowns had come over from America to add to the two or three hundred from over here. On the Sunday morning the big top was packed with clowns and their families as well as local people. It was 1 April, All Fools' Day – how appropriate! But it was also Passion Sunday in the Church's calendar, when the Church recalls the crucifixion. So we had to try to do something about that, it seemed to me. We had a series of skits and stories interspersed with hymns, which was fun and it seemed to be 'going well'. And then we came to the last sketch. I had agonized over it but I didn't see why clowns couldn't portray the crucifixion, so we went for it.

I stepped forward to the lectern and began to read the story of the crucifixion from Matthew's Gospel in straight fashion but was soon interrupted by two clowns who started to tickle me with feather dusters. I protested that they should stop it because this was the serious bit and they shouldn't spoil it. They disappeared and I continued, only to be interrupted again by the same two clowns who started prodding me painfully with the stick ends of their feather dusters. I protested again and off they went, only to come back one final time to grab me by the shoulders and frog-march me into the middle of the ring. I protested innocence and ignorance but one knelt behind me so that the other could push me over his back, and I tumbled on to the floor. They forced my feet together, stretched out my arms, and hammered imaginary nails into my wrists. During their manhandling of me, they also fastened a harness around my waist with a rope attached.

They levered me up to standing and I remained in cruciform position. They taunted as I protested, and then one smashed a custard pie in my face, jeering, 'If you're so clever, who threw that one?' I was then winched to the top of the Big Top as they ran off gleefully, shouting 'April Fool'. I uttered the desperate and desolate cry of 'Why have you forsaken me?' and asked forgiveness for the clowns for they knew not what they did. Still hanging aloft, with the custard pie in my face, I then slumped and 'died'.

After a weighty pause, I was lowered gently down and was received on the ground by two female clowns who very carefully laid me in the centre of the ring, removed the harness, and spread a white sheet over me. They left as a clown one-man-band came into the ring who started to sing 'Lord of the Dance' in his rather cracked and husky voice. Everybody who wasn't too choked by it all joined in and then in the last verse, when it came to the line, 'They cut me down and I leapt up high, I am the Life that will never, never die', up I jumped and started to cavort around the ring. Well, everybody just cheered spontaneously as they sang – it really was profoundly moving and exhilarating, and lots of clowns jumped into the ring to join the dance. Somehow we had captured both the tragedy and the comedy of the crucifixion and resurrection in such a way that many of those there could connect with it and make it their own. They had somehow witnessed it for themselves. We couldn't have done that in church, that's for sure, not least because of the practicalities of the mechanics of hoisting me up. It was precisely because it was in the circus tent and it was the clown being crucified that the whole thing hung together and made perfect sense. It was amplified by the presence of so many clowns in the congregation who inevitably identified with it even more. It had been an enormous risk to re-enact the crucifixion quite so boldly, but it confirmed my belief that clowns have to deal in tragedy as well as comedy, that you can't have one without the other. It also firmly established my desire to have services in circus tents when possible because worship takes on a whole new meaning and dimension, not least when it keeps us on the edge of our seats.

We did try to repeat the same scene the following year, by special request and because the convention fell on the same Sunday, but it wasn't quite the same. I guess we'd lost a bit of that extreme nervous energy that gave it such an edge on that first occasion, and the whole scene was much less of a shock to the congregation this time – many of them knew what was coming. But it was still powerful and challenging in ways that the ordinary reading of the crucifixion can never really be. Familiarity breeds contentment rather than contempt – we're so happy and familiar with the story that it has no effect at all. But take the story into the circus and you never know what happens next . . .

And yet, of course, that isn't true, for the more we go to the circus the more we realize that the clown is always crucified, or at least Auguste is. He is constantly put to the sword by those who deem themselves his betters, down he goes again and again under blows that would surely maim if not kill. We cannot really stop him taking our sins upon him, not least the sin of taking ourselves too seriously, partly because we are grateful for him doing so, grateful that he can do all of this on our behalf. But whatever happens to him, he always bounces back or bounces back up, ready for more. The bouncing is crucial to the clown. If I do a fall on the floor, I have to bounce back up, at least with my head and shoulders, so that people are reassured that I'm not hurt, that we can still play on. If I stay flat out, with my head resting on the floor, the assumption is that I really have hurt myself, and there's no fun in that for anybody, least of all me. I came across a saying of Confucius that rings bells in this connection: 'our greatest glory is not in never falling, but in rising every time we fall.' I don't know what his context was but in terms of clowning, the fact that the clown keeps 'coming back to life' so joyfully has made him a symbol of resurrection for many, never more so than when he's in that vulnerable place, the ring. So although the clown is always crucified, and nearly always crucified on our behalf, there is always resurrection and there is always ultimately final if humble triumph.

The perception of the clown as a Christ figure is not uncommon either. At the Rochester Diocesan Conference already referred to, Dr Richard Burridge, in his summing up of the Conference, expressed his thanks that I had been the Christ figure for him that week, and admitted that it had been 'really good to have someone to be the Christ for us, to play the fool, and to tell us the truth'. A woman priest from the Diocese wrote to express heartfelt thanks that I had been for her the Christ in Gethsemane during the week, and there have been similar sentiments expressed on other occasions. But here is the fool, the clown, on the margins, both despised and lauded, ready to leap in when needed, worldly and yet otherworldly, outlandish in costume, strange in face, recognizably human and yet infinitely more so, here for a while and then gone but never forgotten, walking the knife edge, provoking gales of laughter in pursuit of truth, full of nonsense that makes perfect sense.

There is an otherness about clowns that sets us apart, that makes us holy, so that all clowns may be seen as holy fools. The opposite is also true. The clown has long been suspected of being of the devil, especially in more puritan times. Laughter and mischief were not seen as saintly virtues, and the travelling fools were not deemed worthy of being buried in hallowed ground. Even now some Christians object to having a diabolo in church – a spinning top manipulated by string – and if they must have it, it has to be called something else! Yet I do a story of Simeon in the temple who plays with his diabolo at the temple door, saying 'You've got to keep your whiphand over the devil so he knows who is his master. Up he goes and down he comes, he knows who is his master.' That wouldn't work if I had to change the name! Mind you, I haven't tried taking devilsticks anywhere because I'm no good at devilsticks, and maybe that's just as well! The fact that some children are desperately frightened of clowns may point to the same basic fear that he is an emissary of the devil, a harbinger of evil spirits, and definitely not to be trusted. Burglars and bank robbers have on occasions dressed as clowns to perpetrate their crimes in order to disguise themselves, and the whiteface disguise can be terrifying. But show me a good auguste and I'll point to holiness. Clowns have that sacramental possibility that makes them channels of God's grace, signs of divine hope and inspiration, as well as sources of divine wisdom. The circus is their natural home and habitat.

How about putting St Peter into the Big Top?! He is a classic example of the holy fool and, indeed, the auguste. One moment he's chosen to be the rock on which the Church will be built, the next he's being accused by Jesus of being Satan and of being a stumbling block. Poor old Peter keeps getting it hopelessly wrong and gloriously right. He's a bit of a stumbling blockhead really! Who but a fool would not only attempt to walk on water but manage it, albeit briefly? In the midst of the vision on the Mount of Transfiguration, Peter wants to build three chalets for them all, presumably so they can keep coming back for their summer holidays or be a tourist sensation. One moment he denies three times that he's even met Jesus, the next he avers his love for him three times. One moment he's complaining that he can't heal, the next just the shadow of his cloak does the trick. It seems that Peter is fine until he applies his brain to the subject or till he realizes what he's actually doing. The clown lives by instinct and acts on instinct, reacting and provoking, revelling in spontaneity. If I picture Peter in the ring he would be just like the leading auguste with the Rastellis clown troupe – huge, affectionate, playful, contrary, boundless in energy and reckless in intent, but you know he'll get there in the end. Perhaps it was inevitable that the fool who turned the world upside down by being the somewhat rocky rock on which the Church was built, should himself be turned upside down in crucifixion at his death. But this improbable hero gives all disciples hope, for while we can never do as well as he did neither can we do as badly! Or can we?

The original apostles were a motley lot, not really the stuff of which bishops and important religious leaders are made. It was Judas, the one who was the most earnest and probably the most politically correct, who betrayed Jesus. Saul had to become Paul before he could establish the faith amongst the Gentiles. We did a weekend in Lacock at the end of January in about 1993, and the church was commemorating the conversion of St Paul. As part of the Sunday service some of the youth group did an enactment of that conversion, so we had two teenagers of similar size and build, one dressed as Whiteface, one as Auguste. Whiteface was, of course, Saul rampaging around. When it came to the point of conversion, he disappeared behind the centrally situated screen where the auguste version was hiding, and Auguste came out the other side as St Paul. It worked beautifully because it showed the huge change that came over Paul in his conversion, from the slick and self-important, persecuting Pharisee to the humble evangelist happy to count himself the lowest of the low and complete a complete volte-face.

Another more famous example of the correctness as well as the uprightness demanded by the Church of its disciples, never mind its leaders, is *Red Noses*, a great play written by Peter Barnes and set in the time of the Great Plague in England. The unlikely hero is a priest called Father Floti, who becomes a clown and gathers around him the most unlikely lot of fellow performers, including, most memorably, a blind juggler who keeps wanting to juggle sharp knives! But they bring the hope and light of both laughter and simple faith into the dark, disease-ridden places in ways that nobody else could or would dare to. As the threat of plague recedes, Floti is betrayed and the self-seeking and self-satisfied Pope is given the excuse to dispense with the performers' services as quickly as he had once applauded them, and the Church gets back to taking itself seriously. The heavies move back in with a vengeance. But just for a while, when the need was greatest, it was the clowns who, in true circus style, had leapt in when the emergency had arisen, sorted everything out, made people laugh, and then disappeared again when the emergency was over, leaving the people wanting more and waiting desperately for them to come back. Just for a while they had been signs of the love of the God who suffered alongside them and risked all to do it, stepping into the most vulnerable places to express that love and compassion.

The musical *Godspell* has Jesus as a clown figure. I went to the second night when it opened at The Round House in London, with David Essex as Jesus. I didn't realize beforehand that it had a religious theme! My mother had got tickets so I took my girlfriend of the time, Fiona, and we had good second row seats. Well, it was a revelation. Here was Jesus telling stories and parables with great humour and zest, and an unlikely bunch of disciples who had no idea what they were letting themselves in for. I loved it! Strangely enough, when it came to my college sermon six years later, I didn't make those connections immediately, inasmuch that I didn't quote *Godspell* as an example, but it must have made an impact and been underlying my developing thoughts and theology as I strived to work out what I really did believe.

The picture of Jesus that resonates with me is, as I intimated earlier, this glorious clown figure who turned upside down both the religion of the day and people's understanding of God. For such temerity he had to be crucified, because lined up against him were all the whitefaces in the shape of the lawyers, scribes and Pharisees. They tried to trick him with coins and riddles but he'd only reply with a quip and the truth. They tried to quieten him down, but he chose his own silences. He taught like no one else had ever taught, and he did so with great authority. He told stories that allowed people to see for themselves, usually with such humour that people got the joke. Coming to faith is like getting the joke. To begin with we're excluded and we don't understand, but we're carried along by the story, surprised by the punchline, and suddenly we see, suddenly we know what it's all about, and there are gales of laughter or simply wry smiles as we wonder why we didn't get it before. That seems to me to be a model of Jesus's teaching. His stories are filled with absurd characters, like the debtor who has his big debts wiped out and then throttles the man who owes him but a few pence, sending him to prison until he repays the last penny. There's the outcast Samaritan who wisely doesn't follow the fine example of the lawyer and the Pharisee but rather helps out his fellow human being with acts of kindness and generosity. There's the lovely tale of the preposterous Pharisee and the humble tax-collector going into the temple to pray. The prodigal son has a whale of a time till he ends up eating the pig's dinner, so he returns home to feast on the fatted calf, much to his elder brother's disgust. But these are the characters of the Kingdom of God. It is the tax-collector, the disco-dancer, the outcast and the servant who are held up as models of discipleship, not the Pharisees and the whitefaces who keep their intolerant noses firmly in the air. There must have been much mirth when Jesus told his tales – it was the way he told them.

Once we allow the possibility of wit as well as wisdom in the teaching of Jesus, then the light of humour sheds a completely different and warm light on cold familiarity.

When *Songs of Praise* was broadcast on BBC 1 on 1 April 2001, it was done with almost a hundred clowns in the congregation. Alexis and Tweedy did the story of the Pharisee and the tax-collector as a slosh act, with buckets of slosh flying all over the place, but the point was made and the story was told as Alexis the whiteface was humbled and Tweedy the tax-collector exalted. Once we start to look at the gospel with the eyes of humour or simply the eyes of the clown, it changes things.

When Patrick Forbes celebrated twenty-five years in the priesthood it was the week before Christmas and he wanted me to come and do something at the service. I did the gospel for the day, which was all about the angel Gabriel telling Mary that she was with child and that it was of the Holy Spirit. I attached some huge wings to a garish jacket, careered down the aisle on a unicycle, crashed into the pulpit, and climbed into it to answer the phone, which was of course a call from God. God was giving me instructions about telling Mary that she was pregnant, and I was incredulous about the whole scenario – it was vergin' on the ridiculous! In the end, of course, I did what I was told because I had to admit that the foolishness of God is much wiser than our wisdom. At the end of the service, one of the church wardens came up to me and said that he'd been listening to that story for over sixty years but that today had been the first time that it had made sense. He was enormously grateful! It's back to the notion of embracing the absurdity of it all and then being free to believe. The madness of the gospel is that Mary believed; and even madder the fact that Joseph did too!

Once we blow off the dust of ages and of reverence from the pages of the Bible, we begin to see more clearly. We can choose to reduce the gospel to what we think is both sensible and palatable and can be taken seriously. So a camel can just about squeeze through a gap in the city walls, and that's how difficult it is for a rich man to enter the Kingdom of Heaven: not too tricky with a bit of a push! Or it's as impossible as for that camel over there to get through the eye of that seamstress's needle ... Do we allow Jesus a sense of humour or not? In true clown style, there is extravagant exaggeration simply to make the point, and in the laughter the truth is perceived. At the same time we realize that faith isn't just a laugh, that the demands are great, the path narrow.

It remains a narrow path because both clowns and disciples are called to live on the knife edge between comedy and tragedy, death and resurrection, laughter and tears. Clowns and disciples are suffering servants as well as joyful messengers. The God of whom we speak is a God of vulnerable love, the crucified one who is yet risen from the dead. It's very easy to keep Christ hanging on his cross, where we can see him, and live terribly martyred and long-faced lives; but that doesn't allow for resurrection nor for him suddenly popping up when you least expect him. The Church is much better at observing Good Friday than celebrating Easter. For me, God is the God of tears, who laughs with us as well as cries with us, sharing our sorrows as well as our joys; and he also laughs for us when we don't feel able, and weeps for us when we've no tears left. He's the God I can shout at and share a joke with, whom I stand in awe of and am embraced by, who demands nothing and everything from me.

Clowns speak of comedy and tragedy just by who and what they are. Tears are their trademark too. I was talking to a man in an open prison who had done the highwire in his younger days and had worked at Blackpool Tower Circus for a number of years with the great Charlie Cairoli. Cairoli had said to him that there is always a teardrop on a clown's face because there are always tears as well as laughter. This man didn't know what he meant until he had to fill in as clown one day, and the more he clowned, the more he realized the truth of it. He said that sometimes tears used to pour down his face just at the sight of some of those children, but he'd brush them away and make a joke about it. He admitted he hadn't been very good at it, but that it had been the most satisfying as well as the hardest job he'd ever done – and there was a tear in his eye as he told me.

I'm often asked about the tragic dimension of the clown, whether we aren't all lonely and tragic heroes who when the greasepaint comes off are prone to dive into depression, cry our eyes out or end up broken-hearted. It is the Pagliacci syndrome where the public and the private personas are wildly different, and it is true that the greasepaint can hide a multitude of things. Tony Hancock, the great British comedian of the 1950s and 1960s, who ended up committing suicide in Australia, is another one held up as a possible example. But it's not true of many clowns, if any, because we have not only to keep bouncing back up but also be brave enough to keep bouncing between laughter and tears, between the heights and the depths, and be equally at home in both. The worst place for a clown to actually die is in the ring – it breaks all the rules. Tommy Cooper, that hilarious comedy magician and one of my comedy heroes, collapsed and died on stage in the middle of a routine. The audience thought it hilarious, and assumed it was all part of the act as the curtains closed over his prone body. But his part of the show couldn't and didn't go on, and I guess the tears of laughter turned to tears of grief. The show has to go on – there must be resurrection or at least the hope of it.

If I do my job properly I make people laugh, help them

to cry, and teach at the same time. Clowning works at so many different levels at the same time, from the most simple to the most profound. Clowns aren't just for children, that's for sure, but clowns do allow everyone to be childlike. One of the joys of circus, and even of family services in my experience, is that the kids give the adults permission to play. So the adults shout and laugh and scream and wonder and eat candyfloss and suspend their adult cynicism and world-weariness. We get caught up in the story and revel in the atmosphere. And because the adults behave like that, everybody can. It's all the clown's fault, really. He's the catalyst and focus of our hopes and dreams. But he knows, as Jesus knew, that we all have to be like children if we are to enter into the Kingdom. If we choose to be terribly adult about it, the clown will wonder why we came. But he'll continue to hope against hope that by the end we'll know and that we'll carry away with us a bit of the circus, a bit of his kingdom, in our hearts. And once the sawdust has got you, you've had it! You'll be back, because it's the sawdust that has the sacramental quality, the sawdust that's in the blood, the sawdust that smells suspiciously of God.

4

The Feast of Fools

They didn't have circuses as we know them in the Middle Ages nor did they have clowns in churches, but widespread in Europe was the practice of celebrating the annual Feast of Fools. There is no agreed date of when it happened, partly because, I guess, customs varied from one country to another, and partly because I don't suppose that they had to put it into the church registers together with the amount taken in the collection. But a popular date seems to have been the suitably ludicrous Feast of the Circumcision of Our Lord, which took place on 2 January. On the Feast of Fools a boy was made bishop for the day and the clergy were banished. They burned smokey old boots instead of incense, ate black puddings instead of wafers; they played dice on the altar and games in the sanctuary; they had a donkey in procession up the aisle and brayed the versicles and responses. Everything was turned upside down. A riotous time was had by all, apart from the important people and the ecclesiastical dignitaries, and nothing and nobody was safe from lampooning. Traditionally it started with the line from the Magnificat, 'He hath brought down the mighty from their seats and exalted the humble and meek', and then the Feast began. It would last the whole day, but then the next day everything would revert to normal and everyone would be satisfied.

They could only do it, however, because their faith was

simple and strong. In no way were they lampooning God, they were simply lampooning the Church and gaining a truer perspective in the process. They knew that you have to take God seriously even if he is a God you can share a joke with. But they also knew that you mustn't take religion too seriously – it's just the trimmings and the trappings, the way that we happen to worship in a place that we choose to worship in or find convenient to worship in or have to worship in. In those days, however, there was very little choice either of whether or where to worship – you couldn't jump into the car and be eclectic! What they also knew was that you must never take yourself too seriously, because if you do, you get in the way and God can't get a look in. What the Feast of Fools helped to do was to oil the wheels of that process, so for one day in the year they could forget about themselves in church, do exactly what they wanted to do, express their emotions and vent their frustrations, and then settle back into the comfort and security of their well-practised routines and the hierarchical structures that made up church life. Church in those days was even more of a spectator sport than it is now, so this was a chance to muck in and they revelled in it, while keeping God central to it all. They were, after all, only following his example.

But then along marched the Puritans and the Reformers, and they trampled over these frivolous excesses. Play had no place in a Protestant work ethic, and authority became absolute and sacrosanct. They didn't seem to mind that all work and no play makes Church a dull Church! Consistent with the abolition of the Feast of Fools were the developments that made buildings plainer in decor and services bare of ritual. Church was to be taken seriously, and there were to be no distractions and certainly no theatre. When I was still a vicar in Tooting, one of the local clergy was very supportive of my clowning and enjoyed it as well as approved of it, but it seemed a bit incongruous since he admitted to me that he'd been to the theatre only twice in the fifteen years he'd been vicar of his parish and he'd been 'caught' both times. Presumably by the dictates of his religious upbringing and teaching, theatre remains something sinful and something far too pleasurable for the likes of Christians to enjoy. It is no wonder, sadly, that I've never been invited to his church!

But I have become a kind of travelling Feast of Fools. Once I've been to a place, it's never quite the same again. In my very early days full-time, back in 1992, I went to a church in Bristol, and the vicar wrote to me afterwards saying there had been a huge sea-change in the congregation, and that they were now doing and seeing things he didn't think they would have done for another ten to fifteen years. That to me was extraordinary. My clowning then was still fairly basic, I was still finding my way. Now I am far more polished and, more importantly, more experienced, which makes all the difference. Now I have a slackrope frame and a routine which I call my Slackrope of Faith, which I have done hundreds of times. Then I tied a rope between a pillar and the ironwork at the front of the chancel! I've no idea what I did but it made a difference. It turned things upside down. Once something's been turned upside down or inside out or even both, it's bound to go back in a different way because we've suddenly seen it in a different light, in a different position. Sometimes you find that upside down is actually the right way up, at least for the present.

I went to an ancient church in Sussex in 2000 and it was the first time they'd ever moved the furniture in that historic place, but they made a huge space for me to perform in the middle of the church. Many who came that day commented on how good the church looked like that and how it opened everything up. Some thought so before the service, and even more did so afterwards. There was so much space and light, not just architecturally by the space that had been provided but also by what had happened during the service. Space and light had suddenly been discovered in abundance, not just in the building but in the worship and in scripture. Everything was put back in its rightful place afterwards but it's not quite the same now, and I suspect that the vicar is hoping that one day it will always be as we had it that day!

During the course of a service I'll happily clamber on chairs and over altar rails and perch precariously on the pulpit and never come to harm, even if the churchwarden is having fits. But in one church, I picked up this heavy-looking chair that was obviously the one the vicar used, and the leg fell off! No, it wasn't planned! In another church the stuffed dog which I'd just kicked unceremoniously through a hoop cannoned into the large white screen that had been set up for the overhead projector and sent it crashing to the ground. I think I managed to comment that I'd always believed that he who acetates is lost, and the service continued as soon as they had re-erected the screen so that they could sing the next song. Afterwards I was very apologetic but they were delighted – they had a church meeting that night and one of the items on the agenda was whether to replace the screen with a permanent fixture! It's very rare that things like that happen, I hasten to add, but it does go to show what I was taught at Fool Time: there's no such thing as a mistake, merely an opportunity. Accidents will always happen to augustes, but they are merely opportunities not just for me to do something different but for them to do something different too. Clowns make a difference because they present opportunities. The Feast of Fools presents a different perspective and a very different baseline.

In 1994 I went to Rugby School for the week at the invitation of the chaplain. The main task was to lead the confirmation classes for the forty or fifty candidates who had presented themselves, some at their parents' instigation, some of their own volition. That was for two hours each evening, and we had videos, talked theology, played, did circus skills – it was different. But that wasn't all I did. On the first Sunday evening I did my Slackrope of Faith in the service for the whole school; did three morning assemblies during the week; and talked about it all to all of the thirteen- to sixteen-year-olds in their Religious Education classes. I also stayed in costume and character, as far as I was able, throughout the week, and ate in the different houses for each meal – a majority of the school were boarders. It was a heavy workload.

For the first couple of days as I pottered around the school the reactions were mainly what I would have expected from a dominantly male teenage population: a certain amount of derision and an awful lot of amused but patronising bewilderment. Having a clown around in such a macho and privileged environment didn't make sense to them, so the easiest response was to dismiss me as a childish irrelevance who was way beneath them. I felt very vulnerable, but persevered. By the Wednesday you could feel the mood changing, as the pupils got used to the sight and perhaps the idea of me, and an increasing number of them began to understand what I was about in sessions and classes as well as from each other. On the Wednesday evening I had dinner in one of the girls' houses – they only had girls in the sixth form at that stage. I was talking to a girl of about sixteen, or at least she was talking at me. She was bitching away about this and that, and gossiping about who did what to whom and with whom, and what she didn't like about her but what she'd love to do with him – all the usual stuff! Then in the middle of all this she confessed that when I was on my slackrope, she forgot she was in uniform, forgot she was in chapel, forgot she was at Rugby School, and I'd taken her to a place she'd never even dreamed of. She looked a little misty-eyed at this revelation but then snapped back into the regulation muck-spreading.

At the end of the week, a hulking seventeen-year-old asked if he could come and interview me for a project he was doing in what sounded like a GCSE in journalism. He recorded our twenty-minute conversation and seemed happy enough. Then he switched off the machine and confided that, 'off the record', I'd had a huge impact on the whole school – it would never be the same again. He wasn't a Christian or anything, but he was grateful for all that I'd done. That was pretty staggering in terms of response. The following week the seventeen-year-old who'd been in charge of chapel as chapel orderly wrote to me. He was quite a sedate character, tall and thin, fairly strait-laced but with a twinkle in his eye. We'd had a service on our last confirmation class evening when I'd performed and done various things, and he'd been a part of it. He wrote to say how much he'd been moved, especially by that service which had left him in floods of tears, but also by the whole week's proceedings and activity. In all sorts of ways I had helped him more than I could imagine. It wouldn't surprise me if he was ordained now, but that's mere conjecture, just a feeling about him.

As you can tell, it was an extraordinary week at that school, but there's no use in planning things or trying to recreate situations and atmospheres. Clowns have to go with the flow and see where it takes them. I have what I call my Elijah principle. It isn't necessarily the big things that make a difference – the earthquake, the wind and the fire, the slackrope or the sure-fire story – it's the little things, the nod, the whisper, the odd word, the wave, the throw-away punchline, the sharing of a moment. Tiny things can trigger momentous experiences, and it's no good trying to engineer them nor even trying to analyse them. You just have to let things happen. You can help create the atmosphere, as clowns always will, and you can do your stuff as best as you possibly can, but the rest looks after itself. If people are moved to laughter or tears, or from one place to another, then thanks be to God, for the Feast of Fools is at work.

The Feast of Fools speaks of the topsy-turvydom of the Kingdom of God, where the first are last and the last first, the weak strong and the strong weak, the wise foolish and the foolish wise. The clown in all his vulnerability speaks of all of these by his very existence. When I do a circus skills session with kids, we might have a relay race on little four-wheeled pedal machines. It's usually bedlam as they cheer their own team home, but if at the end I cheerily announce that the team who came last are the winners, there is uproar. But why not? Why shouldn't the team who limped home last but enjoyed it and persevered and who perhaps had to endure the taunts of their so-called betters who had finished already, why shouldn't they be pronounced winners? What is a winner anyway? Perhaps we should cue the parable of the labourers in the vineyard and proclaim them all first (and all last) and give them all the same prize, but the 'winners' wouldn't think that fair either. Often in schools it is the kids with special needs who excel at circus skills. Freed from the strictures of logical thought and the structures of academic discipline, they just go for it, succeed, and are suddenly lauded and applauded. Meanwhile the nine-year-old mathematical wizard is still trying to work out the angles and logarithms involved in spinning the plate! If I talk to a class about it all, the wisest words will often come from those whom the teachers least expected to give them – it happens time and again. In the clown's realm and in God's kingdom all are equal, all will fail, but all will ultimately succeed.

At the end of my Slackrope of Faith routine, I always fail miserably to throw my three juggling rings up on to the cross that rather towers above me on the slackrope frame. Encouraged by my advice to aim for the cross because it's the only way, a stream of volunteers have a go at doing it for me, but they are usually equally inept at this strange game of ecclesiastical hoop-la. If someone does manage it, there is great excitement and thunderous applause. Perhaps the greatest example of this was when a fourteen-year-old boy with Downs Syndrome did it. He'd been totally involved throughout, full of bits of advice and chortling with laughter, so when he winged his hoop straight on to the cross he leapt all round the front of the church in great jubilation, arms aloft in triumph, and the applause was deafening. But the same was true of the Bishop of Exeter when he did it at a Stewardship conference and raised his arms aloft in triumph!

Now that we're on to the subject of bishops, there are a few tales to tell! But it isn't just about bringing down the mighty from their seats. Perhaps you'll see what I'm getting at from the following examples. Back in 1988 a group of us from Holy Fools went up to Lichfield Cathedral to take part in a service that followed on from the Lambeth Conference of that year, when all the bishops of the Anglican Communion gather together. There were twenty-four bishops there. In the main service we did a routine, written by Carol Crowther, who was one of the original founders of Holy Fools, which literally revolved around repentance. The routine led up to the suggestion that we all had to turn around in a circle as a sign of our repentance. It was my job to get people doing it, and some of the congregation were being a bit hesitant, so I suddenly shouted to the twenty-four bishops, who were all sitting behind us in serried ranks on the dais, to do it too. Much to my amazement, those twenty-four bishops from all five continents duly obliged and pirouetted gracefully for all to see. They were happy to play and to be suitably penitent in the process. Since then I've discovered that plenty of bishops are happy to play! Some aren't, and I keep away from them, but plenty are. They're not nearly as mighty as we think they must be! They can sometimes get down off their seats of their own accord.

The first Diocesan Conference I ever went to was the Canterbury Clergy Conference. It was held down in Brighton at the university, and the main meeting place was the modern chapel with its tiered seating in a huge semi-circle that surrounds the platform. I didn't know a soul there and had to decide whether to go to the introductory session in my ordinary clothes or to go in costume and character. I plumped for the latter, and got some very strange looks as I headed across the campus towards chapel.

Nobody there knew that a clown was coming to the conference. The archbishop was still very new, so all the clergy had turned up on parade in best bib and tucker, and they were expecting the entrance of the archbishop when I wandered in with my feather duster and started dusting round the important-looking chair that had clearly been put there for the archbishop. There was an obvious murmur from the bemused gathering, and I disappeared off the other side. The theme of the conference was 'Signs for the Times', so I quickly returned carrying a couple of signs, including 'Keep off the Grass', positioned them carefully and dusted them down. By now some people were beginning to chuckle and I had started to interreact with them. Then out of the blue I turned towards them and asked if they would all please stand – I'd never thought of such a thing before! Anyway, all three hundred or so clergy stood up – I was astonished. I thanked them and told them all to sit down again. There was much laughter, some embarrassment, and a bit of huffing and puffing from those who didn't appreciate the joke. Then I saw the archbishop, George Carey, waiting to come in so I dashed to the back and again called for them all to stand. Some of them did, but some of them obviously decided they weren't going to fall for it a second time, until they turned round and saw it was the archbishop and then they shot up! I led him in with my feather duster raised aloft and guided him to the awaiting throne. Then we solemnly bowed to each other, and I dusted him down. There were gasps of horror as well as gales of laughter, but we bowed again, exchanged some repartee, and I processed off once more.

Introductions followed, and then there was a short service consisting basically of a couple of hymns sandwiched round three poems and some prayers. The first poem was by John Donne, who is pretty heavy at the best of times, but this was interminable and read very badly. Organ music followed to aid our meditation. I hoped that the next poem would be an improvement, but it was even worse, so although I have no pretensions to being a poet I made up a seven-line poem about a clown being a sign of who I am and scribbled it on the back of an envelope. The music started to play after the third poem and I walked purposefully to the lectern. The organist spotted me and, to my eternal gratitude, played ball by stopping the music when he saw me in position. I read my little verse and you could have heard a pin drop in the profound silence that followed, until the organist accompanied my exit. The service ended soon after. I had hit the spot, captured the moment, and set the tone for the rest of the conference. None of it had been rehearsed or anything, it was entirely impromptu, but conference delegates now knew that there might be some fun to be had at a conference for a change. They realized that they couldn't take themselves too seriously – if George Carey could play like that, then they had to too. But they also realized that I was there with something important to offer as well. If I hadn't leapt into that vulnerable place and gone with my instincts, none of that would have happened and I'd have been left with all the 'if only's' that fill so much of our ordinary lives. A moment's hesitation means missed opportunities. But it takes two to tango, and the archbishop did so superbly. Thanks to him, the rest of the conference was a real Feast of Fools as I kept leaping in to interrupt and enlighten at will.

I've done a number of things with the archbishop over the years and we make quite a double act! He's always happy to play, and that's partly because he's happy in his own authority and doesn't feel threatened by me. It's the people who are unsure of their own authority and who therefore fear that I might take away or detract from or destabilise the respect and authority that they do have who find me a problem – it's true of several suffragan bishops I can think of. But bishops and clowns belong together as much as the king and the jester, for they complement as well as need each other. Bishops need chaplains to assist them, but they need a jester even more. When Robert Hardy was enthroned as Bishop of Lincoln he had a jester to lead him in to remind him of his mortality. People in power need that reminder constantly, and the clown can provide that as well as make the bishop laugh, be a shoulder for him to cry on, and be the one who's allowed to speak the truth to him in ways that nobody else can or would dare to. When the bishop and clown are in harness, their power and powerlessness are interchangeable. At the Edmondsbury and Ipswich Clergy Conference in 2000, instead of doing a show as such I was asked to lead a service, so we did a modern day Feast of Fools. My feather duster antics were already familiar to the assembled company, so when the bishop, Richard Lewis, took the feather duster and led me in, it provided great mirth but it also maintained the Feast of Fools traditions. I led him out at the end!

I've custard-pied eight or nine bishops at this point in time. The first one of all was Jim Thompson, the Bishop of Bath and Wells. This was at his diocesan clergy conference too. In the middle of an hour's show, I asked for a volunteer, a biblical wizard, someone who knows his Bible back to front and inside out. Bishop Jim was sitting over on my right in the front row and had been enjoying the show, laughing uproariously, and there were loud cries from several quarters suggesting that he should be my volunteer. Up he came and I sat him on a little red fisherman's stool – I told him it was the first bishop's throne, which hadn't occurred to me till then. I loaded two plates with shaving foam and warned him there were ten simple questions, and if he got them all right, there'd be no problem, but if he got one wrong, he'd be in trouble. I stood behind him with plates perilously poised as he answered the first nine questions correctly. The first nine are easy, like Who built the Ark? But the last question is, What is Matthew 5, verse 39? Nobody has ever got the answer yet! I asked him if he wanted a clue. He said he did, so I pushed one of the custard pies into the side of his face. 'I've got it', he roared. 'Let those who have ears, let them hear'. 'No!', I replied, pushing the other custard pie on to the other side of his face. 'It's Turn the other cheek!' The bishop was convulsed with hysterical laughter, slipped off the chair and rolled on the floor. He had to be carried off! 'Turn the other cheek' is the first principle of slapstick. It not only works, it's biblical. After the conference the bishop wrote and thanked me for all that I'd done over the three days, but especially for the custard pies which had allowed his clergy to see him as clergy ought to see their bishops from time to time. He's quite right, of course!

The good thing about the Feast of Fools is that it may well bring down the mighty from their seats, but it certainly exalts the humble and meek. If a bishop is meek and humble enough to play, he will be exalted, no matter how much his face is covered in custard pie. At the Rochester Diocesan Conference I did the same routine as an introduction to a Bible Study. I hadn't planned on asking Michael Nazir-Ali, the Bishop of Rochester, to be my volunteer, but there he was in the front row, and up he came. I have to admit it was fairly hard work, but it was fun and funny, and the Bishop played along up to the last question. He got his clue, the first custard pie, but gently raised his arm to stop the second one arriving. He's the only one who's ever done that but it didn't matter. He'd played, he'd been custard-pied, and for many people in that diocese he rose considerably in their estimation. Hitherto many had thought of him as a distant and remote bishop, an academic who travelled widely. The custard pie changed that. Here was a man of play as well as prayer, and a large picture of him getting custard-pied was printed on the front of the Diocesan newspaper. Well, it makes a change from a picture with cope and mitre!

I seem to remember swapping my Canterbury cap for the Bishop of Norwich's mitre, at his instigation. David Smith, when a suffragan bishop in Canterbury, was happily addressing a large number of assembled pilgrims with his chin resting happily on the backs of his hands as he held the top of his crosier, when I just knocked the bottom away from the floor and he stumbled forward with a chuckle. The same bishop, when he moved up to Bradford, was introducing his six hallowed fellow bishops at a post-Lambeth Conference celebration in 1998 and then introduced me as the man he'd vote for as the next Archbishop of Canterbury! We've had prince bishops galore in the past in all their pomp and circumstance, but I doubt whether we'll ever have clown bishops. At the actual Lambeth Conference of 1998 I was invited to spend a couple of days with the bishops' spouses, who were having a concurrent conference of their own. A number of the bishops were extremely jealous about this and several bemoaned the fact that I wasn't at their conference and that I wasn't there for the whole three weeks' duration. It might have added a different dimension to their gatherings as well as lightened the burden of their heavy debates. It might have a brought a few of the mighty down from their hobby horses and soapboxes, never mind their seats! The clown brings humility not humiliation, and humour brings with it a new perspective. Because the clown is a mirror to us all, we are at last enabled not only to see ourselves as others see us but just occasionally to see ourselves as perhaps God sees us, and that's a very salutary experience, especially for those burdened with power and authority. It's even more dangerous for a person to be granted the semblance of divine authority. Perhaps all bishops should be consecrated on the Feast of the Circumcision of Our Lord!

There is a great need for the clown in places where you can't see the wood for the trees. There is a great need for the powerless fool to exercise his imagination amongst those who are far too accustomed to wielding power. There is a great need in any gathering for the clown's creative anarchy, for if we accept his invitation we discover that the Feast of Fools is indeed a heavenly banquet and our fellow diners are a motley lot, gathered from the highways and byways and not one of them with an official printed invitation or special headgear. Top table is a sight to behold! 'Come, sit higher up,' is the biblical injunction to the humble and meek, and up they come with some trepidation. Those who originally deem themselves worthy of top table discover the opposite and are less than delighted as they curse the Lord of Misrule, who they blame for getting everything upside down, and thus wrong. But perhaps St Paul's words to the Corinthians need recalling once more: the foolishness of God is much wiser than our wisdom, the weakness of God is much stronger than our strength.

As far as the scribes and Pharisees were concerned, Jesus was the Lord of Misrule, threatening anarchy and order, turning everything and everybody upside down and inside out. This wasn't how religious leaders, never mind Messiahs, were supposed to behave. As for his followers, they were a real motley lot – it was only Judas who might get their official seal of approval ... The fact that he was crucified showed up his pretensions for what they were. Now that the troublemaker had got his come-uppance, peace and order could prevail. But such is human logic, not divine wisdom. Crucifixion didn't signal or signify failure, at least not the failure of Jesus. Of course, it signals the failure of mankind to perceive the Godhead or cope with the reality of the God incarnate, but in the folly of crucifixion the love and the victory of God were confirmed and revealed.

When the clown is accused of being the Lord of Misrule, it is generally only by those who are in charge themselves, the Fat Controllers who remain so fond of status that they can only cope with and thus demand the status quo. Nothing else will do. Enter the clown stage left and you're in trouble. Enter the Holy Spirit stage right and you've had it! For some of those present at the Rochester Diocesan Conference, I was the Lord of Misrule, threatening order, status, solemnity and comfort. But it was necessary! And we moved on. Surely neither faith nor order, both of which we hold so dear in the Anglican Church's domain, can ever remain totally static. The Holy Spirit keeps us moving.

Some people would have us believe that the Holy Spirit keeps us marching in that rather triumphal way that keeps us going in a straight line, clad of course in the armour of God, ten abreast, platoon upon platoon, trampling upon any who dare to get in our way. I'd like to delete all military metaphors from all our hymnbooks, and indeed from our language. I remember taking part in an evening missionary event in Somerset a few years ago. There was the obligatory music group and me. I did all my stuff in slots between the songs and hymns. I seem to remember that it was approaching Holy Week and Easter, and I did some gentle stories as well as playful and manic routines. But all the music was so triumphal, and the exhortations from the worship leader so at odds with all that I was trying to do and say and stood for, that at the end I just stood there and said so. I said something about crucifixion, something about clowns being vulnerable lovers, and that my costume was my armour of God – it didn't make me invincible, it did the opposite in making me totally vulnerable. I felt quite battered and defeated, if you'll excuse those military metaphors, and was simply trying to be truthful and say the thing I thought needed saying. A number of people came up afterwards and expressed their gratitude, not just for all my performance but for those words at the end because I'd turned the whole thing on its head and voiced the fool's perspective. It would have been wonderful if I'd been able to ride a real donkey down the aisle – that would have said a lot. But I think their messianic principles would still demand a stallion or a charger. It takes a fool to know they've missed the point, a clown to have the courage to mention it.

One of the characteristics of my clowning is that it plays with failure. Much comedy is based on failure, often repeated failure. As long as success comes along in the end, even if or perhaps especially if it's not the successful conclusion that we had anticipated, it works. Comedy needs success for its dynamic – theologically, crucifixion must always be followed by resurrection. But failure is more fun. It's a lesson that needs to be learnt in today's society where success is deemed the only yardstick for approval. As I've said earlier, one of my standard punchlines if not catch phrases is not, 'Smile, God loves a cheerful giver', but, 'Smile, God loves a cheerful failure'! It is at the heart of the gospel message, for it is the rich, the successful, the ambitious who have the camel's trouble in squeezing through the eye of a needle in order to get into the Kingdom of Heaven. But then the Kingdom of Heaven is not something that's bought or acquired or collected or stored away in a bank vault for future use and indeed security, it's not something that you can force your way into; it's something that happens, it's an unwarranted gift, a suddenly opened door, a sometimes totally unsolicited membership of a totally inclusive club to which neither perks nor strings are attached. Faith is something that's stumbled upon. Why can't we stumble in the light of God rather than march in it, and bid a hasty retreat at the first hint of a Christian war?! I'd rather tune in to the love of

God and the laughter and tears of heaven than hope to hear the distant wardrums of the Church Militant on the march. Please, go backwards, Christian soldiers! When I was a child, I was always told, 'Soldiers don't cry', if I burst into tears or even if my eyes went watery. If that is the case, then there really is no way I can be a soldier of any description. I'd rather play games and risk tears, tread softly and trip up from time to time.

The only game that some clergy like to play, and these won't play any other, is the numbers game. I am sometimes flabbergasted when a vicar comes up and bombards me with facts and figures about his highly successful congregation. Success in the Church is defined by the number of bums on seats, if they are to be believed. Great catalogues of statistics show how many people came to which service and how many more than the previous year, and certainly how many more than the previous vicar attracted. It's a very easy trap to fall into – I've been there myself! It's a mixture of ego trip and self-justification. But I have always thought that where two or three are gathered together, that's enough. Fortunately Jesus didn't say, Where two or three hundred are gathered together, there am I in the midst. Better still, he didn't say two or three thousand! In June of 2000, all the churches in Swindon gathered at Swindon Football Ground, and it was great to perform on the pitch with a congregation of four or five thousand people. I dine out on the story because I guess it makes me sound good and successful, not because I'm boasting of the things and power of God. St Paul wouldn't be very pleased with me and he would no doubt remind me that another week I might be in a small prison chapel with six or seven people. It doesn't matter, you see. In reality, the prison congregation are no less important than the Swindon crowds just because there are fewer of them. Numbers don't matter, however much they encourage us in our ministry. I get constant apologies from hosts of events who think that they have failed because not enough people have turned up. It's a nonsense. It's a Feast of Fools, not a gathering of the sophisticated and successful with a minimum number requirement.. Of course it's fun with lots of people, not least because people give themselves permission to play far more readily under cover of the crowds, but you just have to go for it and play in the moment with and for the people who are there. You can't worry about people who aren't.

The only failure can be mine, if and when I fail to connect with all the assembled company. There have been times when I think I've failed horribly. I remember a posh school in Horsham where I arrived late and then had to face about a hundred fourteen-year-olds, all boys. Now, the worst possible audience a clown can have must be exactly that. It's not so bad if there are girls too, but all boys is bad news. In my experience, getting there late is the best possible recipe for a disaster. There's no time for anything, let alone preparation or focus, and everything goes wrong. Well, that event just didn't seem to work at all – I felt like a Christian being fed to the lions! We didn't make connections and there was a kind of brickwall response. I may be totally wrong about that, but that's how it felt.

Another occasion was on a Maundy Thursday in a church in a rather deprived area of Bristol. I'd confirmed during the week that it was a seven o'clock kick off and I duly got there at six o'clock, only to find two hundred people sitting waiting for me to start. They'd changed the time without telling me! I frantically tried to set up all my props, attempting to be surreptitious in hiding things they weren't supposed to see, then dashed to the back and changed as quickly as possible. I reappeared as calmly as I could, trying not to be the guy who'd just set everything up so wildly only minutes before, and started the show. I never had a chance! All the kids were gathered at the front while the parents watched on from the back, and the kids were baying for blood. It was hard to deliver the lines above the noisy bedlam of the front three rows. In the end I brought the slackrope in early, thinking that that would get them, that I might assert some control. But that didn't get them. In the end I stopped the show early and admitted that I'd had enough, that I'd failed, but that clowns have to be crucified too. As at the church in Somerset, I said something about vulnerable lovers, but this was an admission of defeat rather than a cry of protest. What I hadn't reckoned on, however, was that lots of them were enjoying it enormously, even the parents who seemed to be chatting away at the back. They weren't familiar with the culture of live performance where people are quiet and involved and respond appropriately and do what they're told, even without being asked. In their own noisy way they'd had a ball, and many of them were conscious of and grateful for the gospel message they had recognized throughout. Apparently, it hadn't been a failure at all, so you can never tell. I think you can let God turn everything on its head and find the worth as well as endless opportunities. The merit of human failure is that it allows divine interruption. But as long as one person enjoys it, it's fine. If that person is me, that's even better! If I'm enjoying it, the audience will too.

But I'm not there simply to please and to amuse. The Feast of Fools wasn't celebrated just to have a knees-up and a laugh, and it certainly didn't please the authorities. I'm there to challenge and provoke and speak of the things of God. That means I have to risk offence. You have to risk offence in order to push people far enough, to move them towards the next precipice. A vicar from the comfortable suburbs of Surrey wrote to me after a Sunday morning service, saying that three people had been terribly offended by my contribution to the service but that two hundred will never forget the message! That's not a bad ratio. The vicar even admitted that one of the three was the leader of the local Conservative Party, who had probably protested on principle! At least they were there at the service. Some people complain bitterly about me without even seeing me – I don't presumably fit into their religious equations. We nicknamed a woman in New Eltham, 'Our Lady of the Hat'. She came to the service with an enormous hat on, stalked out of church as soon as the clowns appeared – this was in my pre-Fool Time days when a group of us from Holy Fools were doing things – only to reappear when her spies told her the coast was clear to receive communion. It was all pre-planned and stage-managed. There are plenty of Our Lady of the Hats around – a churchwarden in Oxford sat at the back and stuck herself resolutely behind her Sunday newspaper when I was on. I think she must have been listening though because she never turned any pages! Ninety-five per cent of the congregation loved it – it was just the powermongers who couldn't cope.

Rochester Diocese, at that oft-quoted conference, found me terribly difficult to begin with and some were terribly offended, but I reassured the organizers that if they weren't then I wouldn't actually be doing my job. The main bone of contention was that I had led Bishop Jonathan, a huge black African bishop from Kenya, I think, into church with my feather duster. Some of them worried that photographs might be sent back to his Diocese and he might be embarrassed by it – he wasn't at all. It was quite preposterous. Almost all of the protesters and dissenters came round in the end, but we had to work through the sometimes painful and certainly painstaking process to get there. A dean of a Cathedral found me 'nearer to blasphemy than foolishness' and in effect barred me from going back. I don't know what he meant by foolishness but now that he's gone on to even higher things, I've been back several times – and he's still barring people at the new place! He wasn't prepared to take pains to wonder at or work through his own reactions but perhaps we should have spent the time to do it, for both our sakes.

I did a mission with the Archbishop of Canterbury in a group of churches in his diocese. I'd been around schools and other places for three days and it culminated in a service on the Saturday evening. I was to do the first half, George Carey would do the second – a good double act, as I've said before! I played around to begin with, dusting round the place, balancing the churchwardens' staves, reacting to those who were obviously enjoying it all. I led the archbishop in with my feather duster aloft. We sang, and I did my half, including the Slackrope of Faith. The Archbishop then preached for about half an hour and we sang some more. After the service, a churchwarden of one of the group of churches confronted me to say that he thought I ought to know that he had been terribly offended by all my messing about at the beginning of the service, and that he'd been on the point of walking out. But because the Archbishop was coming, he hadn't, for he'd come especially to hear him preach. But he was very glad he hadn't walked out for he admitted that the more I did, the more wonderful he thought it all was, and now he looked at his faith in a completely different way! The Feast of Fools had been at work again. It had turned his faith on its head and yet presented this viable alternative that he was happy to embrace and is no doubt still pursuing to see where it takes him. He could have stopped at the first fence, got four faults for a refusal, and missed out completely. I'm very glad he didn't.

The clown is not just the suffering servant but the subversive servant, who risks all in his attempts to turn both the Church and the world upside down. It takes courage to be the truth-teller in any place at all, but it takes even more courage to speak the truth in those places where people think they already possess it. Only a fool would attempt to! But in my earliest days in a parish I took on board the old axiom that ministry is to do with distressing the comfortable and comforting the distressed. That may sound topsy-turvy, but it's not a bad job description for the clown either.

5

Humour and Healing

At the beginning of the nineteenth century, Grimaldi the Clown was at the peak of his powers. He transformed pantomime, becoming the star of the show. He was the first clown to use greasepaint and is regarded as the father and originator of clowning as we know it today. His comedy was often vulgar and very knockabout, verbal and very physical. At the end of his life he was a very sick man, some of it due to all the pratfalls he had taken. He went to his doctor in search of a remedy. The doctor apologized that he had nothing to offer him, but he could recommend going to see the great clown Grimaldi ... That may well be an apocryphal tale – the same story has since been told of five other clowns to my knowledge – but he was the first! More importantly, it does testify, if not to the healing power of humour at least to the relationship between the two. Grimaldi himself is also credited with healing a sailor who had been deaf and dumb for years after an attack of sunstroke, but who enjoyed Grimaldi so much that both speech and hearing returned. If the last chapter was more about distressing the comfortable, then this chapter is about comforting the distressed.

Humour is to do with wholeness, with togetherness. It is a vital part of being fully human. It's part of this whole area of being able to laugh at yourself, to see the funny side of things, and ultimately to have both hope and faith. *Humus* is the Latin for earth – the Greek dish is spelt differently! – and etymologically, humour and human have that same derivation. Humour earths us. We are but dust and to dust we shall return. Yet laughter offers the possibility of a way of transcendence, of taking us out of ourselves, out of our present predicaments and circumstances, and then bringing us back to see things in a different light. Humour brings perspective, sometimes the divine perspective. I've lost count, not that I was actually counting, of the number of times people have come up to me and said how grateful they were for the laughter. They hadn't laughed so much for years, even since they were a child – and that's an indictment of adulthood. Or it was the first time she'd laughed since her husband died, or the first evening he'd enjoyed since his wife had left him. In Nottingham Prison, a long-haired man came up and thanked me because it was the best night he'd had in seven years. Assuming he'd been in prison for all those seven years, I don't suppose there was much to beat! But it shows what laughter, and what a clown, can do.

I've visited quite a lot of prisons as clown. Between September 2000 and May 2001 I went to thirty-three of them, thanks largely to the Faith and Foolishness Trust which supports my work and ministry. The Trust received a large grant specifically to pay for me to go into prisons and to schools who can't afford me, for prison chaplaincy budgets are even worse than school ones. The prisons are all quite different in that some are open, some closed; some male, some female, some mixed; some for remand prisoners, others purely local, some specializing in vulnerable prisoners; and each has a different category of security. But they're all the same in terms of the needs of the prisoners, for in essentially dehumanizing places there is a crying need for laughter, and laughter, of course, is the great liberator – it brings freedom.

At one prison in the North–East, two officers were assigned to me because the authorities were worried by the props I was taking in. Prisons tend to get twitchy when you want to take ladders and rope inside! Both officers were very stand-offish to begin with. One took one look at my props and then at me, and in all seriousness said to the chaplain who was there to greet me that he was sure the sign outside said that this was a prison. When the chaplain replied that the prisoners there were only human too, the other officer jabbed his finger in the direction of the prison wings and swore that there were no humans in there at all. Anyway, as it happened they were very helpful unloading all the props, and very friendly too. They loved the show – we had to do it twice, once for the ordinary prisoners and once for the vulnerable prisoners who had to be kept separate. The two officers were really involved and laughed uproariously, regardless of the fact that they were with all these prisoners that they apparently despised. At the end they shook me warmly by the hand, wished me much luck, and thanked me for a wonderful morning. They had become more fully human that morning, and at least for a while had enjoyed themselves in the company of other humans who for that short time were their equals. Laughter is a great leveller.

In another prison, there was a tall man in his twenties, quite jaunty and confident, dressed differently from all the others in green overalls with bright yellow patches. He shook me heartily by the hand in gratitude for the service, and I commented on his clothes for they were very like my green trousers which have large yellow pockets. 'Snap!', I cried! Afterwards the chaplain enquired whether I wore patches on purpose. I had no idea what she meant until she explained the significance of that prisoner's green and yellow costume. If a prisoner makes an escape attempt, he is then put in what they call 'patches' so that everyone knows. That morning we could have put them all in 'patches', for they had all escaped, all transcended the prison walls in their laughter and in their engrossment in the service, and maybe it was my green and yellow friend who recognized that more than all the others, for he had made a successful if brief escape at last.

It is a great achievement really to make prisoners laugh, and even more to help them cry. It depends on the regime, of course, and some prisons have much better vibes than others, but it seems to me that laughter and tears are a great threat because they dissolve the defence mechanisms that have been so carefully constructed and seem so necessary to survival in imprisonment. In Winchester prison, a youngish man confessed that it was the first time he'd laughed since he'd been in. I don't know how long that had been, but as he left to go back to his cell he was still smiling. Another prisoner was tearfully grateful that now he could see light in his darkness, that there truly was light at the end of the tunnel. But almost all prison congregations are quite hard to begin with because they have to give themselves permission to respond and react. Faced with a clown, they are hesitant to commit themselves. The easy way out is to laugh at me – there are always a few who make that obvious. But by the end you hope that they're laughing with you, and most of the time that's true. You take them on a journey, help them tunnel out of the prison they've made for themselves, and by the end they're feeling human, sometimes for the first time in years. One prison chaplain at a female prison was so thankful, not least because all the women were able to laugh at such silly things, as she put it. It was the laughter of play, a laughter of childhood – and given the childhoods of many of them, that was miraculous. At that same prison, the last of four services was for the detox unit, and a rather shrewish-looking woman in the front row raised her eyes to the heavens as I entered and said loudly, 'For God's sake, I'm twenty-eight years old.' By the end she was enjoying it!

Laughter, when it is genuine, is the greatest of gifts. Cathartic and cleansing, it is uplifting and resonant with hope. Of course it can be the opposite, cruel and damning, bullying and degrading. There is hollow laughter, polite laughter, and laughter that doesn't quite get the joke. There is the laughter of one-upmanship, the racist jokes and sick jokes and the in-jokes that separate 'us' from 'them', the laughter designed to put others firmly in their place or in the place where we think they belong. There is much humour today that is merely insulting of other people and quite spiteful, especially of the so-called celebrities of society. And it isn't a modern equivalent of bringing down the mighty from their seats because the laughter, like the jokes, is cheap. Genuine humour is more costly. Too often what passes as humour is the equivalent of putting someone in the stocks and chucking rotten fruit or jokes at them. Genuine laughter delights in the other person not their predicament. It's a rather broad generalization, but one difference between a stand-up comedian and a clown is that the clown's humour must always be at his own expense, whilst the comedian's humour is often at someone else's. Healthy humour is never entirely at someone else's expense.

In laughter we should be united not separated. I did a show at Timsbury near Bath, in a full church. A young woman arrived about fifteen minutes late with a small child in tow, and I did the usual gag of looking at her, looking at my watch, looking at her again, and then asking loudly whether she was Church of England. I suppose that makes me a bit guilty of laughter at her expense, but she laughed too – it was shared laughter. She made her way towards the front of the church where there were a couple of seats available, and that made her entrance all the more obvious. I mentioned her again later on and got her up as a volunteer, now that she was here. Anyway at the end of the show she came up towards me and I suddenly thought I might be in trouble, I might have gone too far. But far from it. It turned out that I'd married her – no, it wasn't my wife, I'd conducted the service! It had been five years previously, when I'd been helping at a vicar-less church for three months just after leaving circus school and before I started getting busy. She'd come to thank me for the sermon I'd preached that day.

My wedding sermon only lasts two minutes and it centres upon my clown stole – a stole is the often coloured scarf that many priests wear round their necks. When I left my curacy in Catford, a woman in the parish called Anne Taylor, who sadly has since died, presented me with a white stole with a happy clown face on one end, a sad clown face on the other, and a cross made of teardrops in the middle. I always wear it for special occasions, which is what white stoles are for. The sermon simply gives the advice that as long as the couple learn always to laugh together and cry together, they will be fine. For to laugh alone means something's gone wrong, and to cry alone is quite awful. And if they laugh and cry together, they may even find God amidst the laughter and the tears, for he is himself the God of laughter and tears. I know it's true of my marriage, because laughter and tears are necessary to keep drawing us back together, to keep falling in love anew. The sermon had apparently stood them in good stead too, and indeed she wanted me to come and baptize their daughter. Sadly I couldn't manage the date, but I would have worn the stole for that service too.

Laughter and tears both bring and keep people together. They break down the barriers, dissolve the defences, pour over the ramparts, fill in the trenches, and we suddenly recognize once more our common humanity and even affirm that life is indeed good. There is a kind of nakedness in laughter and tears, for there is nowhere and nothing we can hide when laughter and tears have got hold of us. It's the Adam and Eve experience in the Garden of Eden, for suddenly all those carefully positioned and polished fig leaves, all those carefully crafted versions of ourselves that we've plastered over our real selves in endless layers, all the artificial and superficial bits and pieces that we treasure, they each drop off and all is revealed. And that's scary. But that's why we sometimes need special people to laugh and cry with, for then in the laughter and tears we know not just that we are loved but that we are loved for who we really are, and that's the most affirming thing of all. That's the nature of divine love, after all. It is a good test of authentic friendship as to how much we allow ourselves to cry and laugh together. One of the great privileges of being a clown is that I'm friends for life with thousands upon thousands of children, and even adults as well. They've told me, and you can see it in their eyes too. And I guess it's because we've shared precious moments, we've laughed and cried and played together, and had the time of our lives.

One of the distinctive features about laughter and tears is that ultimately they are irrepressible and uncontrollable, and therein lies their joy and the roots of their healing possibilities. But it also explains why dictators and control freaks and all those who refuse to see the joke find them so threatening. Laughter erupts, we burst into tears. We can't help ourselves. We can't control ourselves when laughter and tears get a grip. People wet their trousers! Laughter is deemed to be infectious or contagious – words we normally reserve for the worst of diseases! Some people are blessed with a laugh that you can't help joining in with even if you haven't got a clue why you or they are laughing. Some years ago I went with my triplet brother Toby to see Rowan Atkinson's one-man show at the theatre. Toby has an extraordinary laugh and he usually manages to control it, but when he does let rip it never fails to get everybody going. Rowan Atkinson was wonderful, and on two occasions during the show Toby really did lose control. You could hear him above everybody else's laughter, so then there was a double dose, a double laugh, because everybody joined in with and because of Toby's laughter. On the second occasion Rowan Atkinson walked to the edge of the stage to find out what we looked like – he probably wanted Toby as a regular, not that he needed it! I'm prone to what is called 'corpsing' – and prone is the operative word. There are times when I find something so funny that I just sink to the floor in mirth – I cannot physically stand up, and I just cry with laughter. Eventually I pull myself back together, but it's a very cathartic experience. I don't think it's an accident that it's called corpsing, because in a very real sense you die in the process and are reborn a different person with a fresh outlook and a clean slate.

Equally, there are times when I can't stop myself from crying, and times when I can't stop crying once I've started. I'm particularly susceptible to films, but also to books and plays. I'm a terrible weepy! I usually try to take the soft option and only watch gentle comedies, but sometimes I'm outvoted by the family. Tales and examples of courage and heroism and sacrifice finish me off. But anyone who has been bereaved and lost somebody close will know that tears creep up on you unawares, often when you least expect them and at the slightest and unlikeliest of triggers. You either then try and swallow them or let them out - the latter is infinitely better!

On the day of my father's funeral, I managed to control myself beforehand until suddenly I had to write something on the little card on the wreath. I couldn't begin to write anything that remotely represented what I needed to say, and I just cried. Somehow my tears said it for me, and I contented myself with something rather less heartfelt and profound in the written word. I cried a bit in the service, but the daft thing about funerals is that there is that English expectation that you control yourself and don't embarrass yourself and other people by bursting into floods of tears. Being English, I more or less complied! But the following Sunday I went to communion at the same church, and I just wept my way through it, from start to finish. I wasn't feeling particularly sad, certainly not for the duration of the whole anglican hour, but it allowed me again to express things I couldn't articulate in the place which was obviously the most appropriate. The vicar obviously spotted me during the service and ran up to me afterwards as I disappeared down the church path, to check that I was OK – and yes, I was, perfectly, thanks to the tears. Tears are nothing to be embarrassed about or to apologize for. It seems to me they are given us by God, and in the silence of our tears we speak volumes in the only way that we can. And again, they wash away some of the worries and fears and stresses that beset us, and give us another chance with a new perspective. If we choose to, we can find God in the tears, just as we can find him in the laughter. Once we lose control, God's got a chance. The simplest way of discipleship is to hand over control to him, but that's much easier said than done!

One of the most interesting developments in the Church in recent years is the phenomenon known as 'the Toronto Blessing'. This was an outbreak, an outpouring, a sudden surge and gift of the Holy Spirit, so called I think because it all started at that most unlikely of holy shrines, Toronto Airport. It has been a big thing in the charismatic churches in this country at least, and many leaders of those churches immediately caught planes and flew out there, returning with this blessing, rather like tourists returning from Brighton with a stick of rock. But what interests me about it all is that the major sign of the receiving of the Spirit in this instance is that you collapse in uncontrollable laughter: you corpse and are reborn. Laughter has rarely been a sign of born-again Christians, for the Church has largely specialized in rather earnest Advent-like joy, but here was a breaking of the mould. Perhaps that playful and elusive Holy Spirit really was gleefully at work, but sadly some people got hold of the wrong end of the stick, not to say the stick of rock, and took control themselves once more. It's easy to be cynical, but there was a tendency for people to get zapped, laugh, become members, and never laugh again!

I spent a very enjoyable and happy weekend at a church in Birmingham, not long after the Toronto Blessing had begun. The vicar had been out there and returned excited. He'd asked me to come in order, I guess, for them all to explore and experience not just laughter but humour too, and all its possibilities and ramifications. It was great fun in what was a thriving church – I assume it still is! On the Sunday evening we finished with a service in which I took my usual part and managed not to repeat anything I'd done already. At the end, the vicar asked me to do the blessing. I announced to the congregation that I would give two blessings, the first of which had been taught me by an old native American I'd met in the United States the previous summer, the second more traditional. We paused reverently for a few moments before I said, 'The first blessing is simply this: Kemo Sabi – the old Tonto blessing.' For a moment there was a slightly stunned silence and I thought perhaps I'd gone too far or perhaps they'd never watched *The Lone Ranger*, but then the whole place erupted with laughter. And in the laughter was the blessing, it seemed to me. This was genuine laughter that laughed at themselves and laughed with God and in the process accepted themselves and accepted God. Genuine laughter is life-giving as well as life-enhancing. It is brimful with health and vitality, and we shouldn't need to get it on prescription.

There has been a lot of research in recent years on the benefits of laughter and its relation to health. There has long been at least a tacit admission that laughter is the best medicine. I have no expertise in the medical field at all but it seems fairly obvious to me that laughter is not just a sign of continued health or a sign of increasing health on the road to recovery. Is it too naïve to hope that the ability to laugh at yourself, and thus accept yourself and not take yourself too seriously, puts an end to hypochondria and must reduce psychosomatic disorders? There seems little doubt that laughter and, I think, tears reduce stress. This is obvious by observation and experience. A good laugh in a tricky situation breaks the ice, reduces the stress, deflates the pressure. In laughter we feel more hopeful, we see things in a different light, and the agonies of only a few moments before become a distant memory. But what medical people are also discovering is that laughter reduces the effects of pain and treats physical pain in a similar way. There are psychological benefits in laughter, as testified by the increasing number of laughter clubs and clinics, but there are purely physical benefits and effects too. Laughter relaxes the body and thus the muscles, slows the heart rate and helps blood pressure. Laughter is good for breathing because, like coughing, it clears the upper respiratory tracts. It is said to improve intestinal and hepatic functions – it gets our insides moving! It calms pain by increasing the amount of endorphins – laughter doesn't just take our mind off pain, it does something physically to reduce the amount we suffer. It has been shown to be good for insomnia – at last people can sleep not just peacefully but contentedly. There is always the implicit suggestion that the more we laugh, the longer we live – we do indeed live happily ever after!

Laughter clubs are springing up all around the place, originally founded by Dr Madan Kataria in Bombay. People gather first thing in the morning and spend fifteen to twenty minutes laughing. Beginning with forced laughter, the session is interspersed with yogic exercises and different ways of laughing. Genuine laughter develops very quickly, and because it is done in community, it appears to work. It seems to me a great way to start the day! Adults lose the ability to laugh, or at least the inclination to laugh, and that's a terminal illness! Children laugh all the time, but the older we get, the more 'adult' we think we are and the less we laugh. Vain as most of us are, we all look in the mirror in the mornings. If we just laughed at what we saw instead of groaned or admired, the face we see the next time might well have changed for the better. Beauty lies in wholeness and contentedness, not in jars of gel and anti-wrinkle cream. Ridiculous as it may seem, we're all beautiful if we allow ourselves to be.

Research into humour in the workplace has reached what seems a very common-sense conclusion that it helps. Just as the clown creates and maintains the atmosphere in the circus so that everything else can happen, so laughter creates the atmosphere in which work can best happen. Laughter is good for morale and for team-building, and thus good for production as well as staff loyalty. It is inclusive, so that people feel a part of it, and it reduces the horrors of stress. Some places have established playrooms or humour rooms where staff can disappear and watch a comedy video or play a game or juggle. Juggling is like laughter in that you can't think of anything else when you're doing it. It's physical and ultimately contemplative as you disappear into its rhythms, so it takes you out of the stressful situation and into a different place, where you can relax and think of nothing at all apart from the objects that keep passing through your hands. Social functions and outings are organized so that staff can relax together, have treats together, get to know each other better. Some firms have monthly playdays specifically for that purpose. Laughter and play help creativity and imagination because they keep bringing us back fresh and hopeful. Work with a smile on its face must provide job satisfaction all round.

I visit lots of schools to do hour-long show/assemblies and sometimes circus skills workshops, as mentioned earlier. But you can tell a happy school almost as soon as you walk in, both by the welcome and certainly by the amount of co-operation and by the amount of staff involvement. In some schools you only get a skeleton staff sitting sentry-like around the edges, some of them desperately trying to mark books, and none of them laughing at all. I still try and win them over. At others, all the staff gather and even some parents too, and they laugh uproariously and all join in. The kids enjoy it in both places but everybody enjoys it more in the latter. My guess would be that the second type of school is not only a happier place but provides a much more complete education and probably produces better results, certainly in terms of the children who leave the place but also in terms of academic results.

I went to one primary school with the warning about the head teacher ringing in my ears. I was told that she was awful, a strict disciplinarian, and feared by one and all. I was greeted by a woman whom I took to be the head teacher and was pleasantly surprised at how friendly she was. I even congratulated myself privately on how well I was handling her! The assembly was great fun, with everybody joining in. At the end of the hour I got three huge and hearty cheers that raised the roof, but then everything went quiet and we could all hear footsteps coming down the corridor. It suddenly became obvious that the head teacher was coming. She was the only person, apart from the school secretary, who had missed the show – the secretary, unlike the head teacher, didn't have a choice. The staff and pupils alike froze as she came in, stared at them coldly, and ordered them to sit quietly on their bottoms. I promptly sat down on the floor with a bump which of course produced barely stifled laughter. The head teacher was not remotely amused and shouted at them all to sit up straight and cross their arms. I managed to sit up straight but failed miserably, despite several attempts, to cross my arms – they just kept slipping through each other! Eventually she restored order, I behaved myself and they all went back to their classes, but I believe as well as hope that that school has never been quite the same again, thanks to the laughter. It seems obvious to me that if you can laugh and play and tear your hair out with your colleagues rather than about them, it's got to be healthier and happier for all concerned.

The most obvious example of the connections between humour and healing is to be found, of course, in hospitals. A lot of research has been done on humour in the hospital as workplace, and how staff operate and co-operate, as well as cope with the high stress that is an inevitable part of working there. Much documented has been the so-called gallows humour that so characterizes hospital humour, where jokes and comments that might seem quite sick and inappropriate to the ordinary person when taken out of context are found to be the basic survival mechanism of both nurses and doctors. Again we see that humour is necessary to put things in perspective. But humour is also necessary to both health and recuperation. Since the mid-1980s clowns have become a familiar sight in our hospitals. In a way, that's nothing new – Coco, as we've said, was a great hospital visitor in the 1950s and 1960s. But since Michael Christensen, a clown working with the Big Apple Circus in New York, established the Clown Care Unit in 1986, clowns have been seen much more as part of the team needed for healing and health rather than just as a pleasant distraction and treat for the children. Michael Christensen now has over seventy clowns working in a number of hospitals in New York, and they visit, and are trained, as clown doctors who do their rounds in the childrens' wards just as real doctors would do. It's all done in consultation with the nursing and medical staff – they are universally regarded as crucial to the team, and the children's anticipation of their visit is eager, to say the least.

The Big Apple Circus are recognized as being the pioneers, but others have followed in their outsized footsteps. The Theodora Foundation employs twenty-six clowns visiting twenty-nine hospitals in Switzerland, and they also founded the programme that sends British clowns to Great Ormond Street Hospital for Children, as well as St Thomas's Hospital and Guy's Hospital. These are seen as clown doctors in the Michael Christensen model. But more popular, especially in the United States, are the large numbers of teams of what are now called Caring Clowns, who visit hospitals and nursing homes and the like. They are not trained to the same degree as clown doctors nor are they necessarily as good at clowning as the Big Apple professional clowns, but they do a wonderful job in very many ways and places. They look good and they do good, and they are trained to abide by certain ground rules dictated both by the hospitals but also by clowning itself. Hospitals don't demand circus-style clowning – most of the time it would be hugely inappropriate and inappropriately huge! Hospitals need a more playful and gentle style of clowning, one that is still funny and provokes laughter but is somehow more collaborative. There's an awful lot of blowing of bubbles by clowns and patients in hospital wards. Bubbles have a rather magical power that somehow helps people connect and yet takes them somewhere else. They have a dream-like capacity and quality that allows us to go off on a journey of our choosing. Clowns in hospitals use all sorts of bits of pocket magic and small props and puppets.

Puppets can be particularly useful because sometimes children will tell things to the puppet that they wouldn't dream of telling a person, least of all one of the medical staff. That's not to say circus-style doesn't have its place, because I'm convinced it does, but as always in the jester's art, you have to get it right – and in a hospital of all places, you can get all sorts of things chopped off if you get it wrong! Caring clowns are world-wide now. I know of clowns from Iceland to Australia who devote their clowning time to their local hospital. The best clowns in all spheres of clowning have always been caring – it's of the essence of clowning. Now it's being recognized more globally and put to more obvious use and effect.

I've done a certain amount of hospital clowning over

the years. Quite a lot of it has been with children, but not all by any means. I think it's a shame that most hospital clowning in the world seems to be restricted to children. It confirms the old prejudice and chorus that 'clowns are for children', but they're not! Children do, however, respond readily, if they're feeling well enough. With any luck, as well as skill, they will certainly be feeling well enough by the time you leave, as long as you haven't outstayed your welcome. As any bedside visitor knows, you're not there to exhaust the person you've come to see, however patient, not to say long-suffering, that person may be!

I remember spending a very happy morning at the children's hospital in Manchester. They didn't know what to expect, but then neither did I! A majority of hospital clowning is purely spontaneous. You just have to react to what's happening and respond to each individual. I was escorted round the wards, and stopped at most bedsides. When you enter a ward, you have to work out immediately who wants to play, who is pleased to see you. Clowning is all by invitation in that you can't force yourself upon an unwilling child. The child is there to play with, not to be your victim! It may be that those who stare at you stonily to begin with warm to the task when they see it could be fun, and then they begin to join in. I often take a couple of spinning plates with me. It's something for them to have a go at, and it's especially good for older children who might not otherwise give you the time of day. In Manchester it was fun. I felt like the Pied Piper on occasions, with little groups of people following me round. The time raced by and I had to leave, having failed miserably to get as far as we'd planned. But the chaplain wrote to me afterwards to say that his abiding memory of a day that will live long in his memory was of the young boy in an oxygen mask who could hardly breathe but had never stopped laughing all the time I was with him, and who had still been smiling all over his face despite that awful mask when he'd gone back later. He was a kid of about nine or ten, who'd played happily with the spinning plates and loved all the bits of slapstick nonsense I'd done, and for once had been doubled up in mirth rather than pain. Perhaps I'd just been a brief but happy interlude in a long and boring, painful day, but even at its lowest level, it made the visit worthwhile.

There's no doubt that a clown is an amusing if passing distraction, but clowns are also used a lot to distract children when a particularly painful procedure has to be carried out. This is normally when the clown is a recognized member of the hospital team and thus a regular visitor who may well have established a relationship and rapport with the child in question. One thing for sure is that you have to be in touch with your own squeamishness or you won't be any help to anyone. I can't stand the sight of my own blood but I'm better with other people's!

Most of my visits to hospitals have been a one-off thing and most of these have taken the form of going round the wards, but in Edinburgh on a visit to the children's hospital I had to do a show in one of their playrooms. I used my breakaway bike amongst other stuff, so retained the circus-style side of it despite the limited amount of room. You have to be careful of fragile limbs and people when your front wheel falls off or when you try and ride it upside down! There were only about seven children and a few parents and nurses, but that was plenty. I discovered the reason why I wasn't asked to go round the wards – they have two clown doctors who do the rounds already. Two trained drama therapists have become clowns. Originally funded by a Trust, for a year I think, the hospital had seen how successful and appreciated their presence has been and now pays for them out of its own budget.

To date, I haven't had the opportunity nor the funding to sustain a commitment to one hospital, and I'm afraid those two factors go hand in hand. But by the time this book is published I should be about half-way through a year's programme of weekly visits to Odstock Hospital in Salisbury. It's being done under the auspices of the ArtCare Department and the chaplaincy, and is being called Clown-Care. There is no explicit evangelistic intent, for I go as clown, as vulnerable lover, to see what happens next. As always in hospitals, I wear a white coat but it has big pockets and multi-coloured braiding. Otherwise I retain my normal costume, including my outsized clerical collar, so people make connections as they wish. This project will build upon a visit I did in 1995, which apparently is still talked about!

I went for a week, and a programme of sorts was worked out in advance, but the emphasis was on being around for staff, visitors and patients alike, whatever age they might be. It was all the impromptu stuff that worked best and did the most good, not the planned content. If a visit was arranged for a particular time, there was usually the expectation that there was going to be a show because that's what clowns do. But that wasn't what I was there for really, as people soon discovered. A last-minute purchase had been a zimmer frame with wheels, on which I draped various outsize or absurd props, such as a stethoscope made out of hosepipe and sink plungers. Together with a set of funwheels, which are a pair of wheels with a crank and pedals in the middle on which you balance and pedal, they made a suitably ludicrous means of transport for careering, albeit rather slowly, round the hospital. Odstock Hospital is a modern one and thus is nearly all corridors with a few wards thrown in! The corridors are extremely wide as well as tortuous, so the transport by zimmer was a godsend for fooling around as I went from one place to another. You can't switch off between wards or assume that people will think you're off-duty and just passing. It worked a treat and created much laughter as well as mayhem in those endless corridors. There were still some who 'passed by on the other side', pretending not to notice this idiot on wheels, or trying to treat it as an everyday occurrence, but for most, as many admitted, it quite made their day. Another daft visual gag was to put on one of those arrow-through-the-heads under my hat and then race up to a bewildered member of staff or visitor and ask the way to the Casualty Department! One ward sister took me very seriously and gave me hurried and detailed directions, totally oblivious to the joke – you can't win 'em all! It keeps coming back to the question of picking the right people to play with. In show terms, it's the knack of choosing the right volunteer. I don't know how many times I've been told that a certain volunteer or a child in the audience was a complete gift. But you have to accept the gift, work on a relationship with the person, and then react and provoke appropriately and creatively. You go with it and hope it works. You know when you've chosen the wrong volunteer – they're even harder work! In the same way, you have to get it right in hospital.

I arrived unannounced in one adult ward, and there was a man in bed in a room of his own just near the entrance. There was a flicker of interest as I pedalled slowly by, so I reversed and just waited by his door. I wasn't invited in, so didn't go in, but he was friendly and wanted to know what all this was about. We had a long conversation and he became quite animated. I didn't do any clowning as such, but it was appropriate on this occasion just to talk and to listen – he talked about himself too, and his predicament. There are times when all you're there for is to talk and, even more important, to listen. There are times when you just sit and hold hands and say nothing at all, but just by being there it makes a difference. Clowns talk to anyone and will spend time with them, because they are foolish enough to touch the untouched and the untouchables, being no respecter of reputations, whether good or bad. We take people at face value and as we find them.

In the end it was time to move on so I pedalled into the main ward. In the first bed on the left there was a woman flat on her back, with her head tilted slightly forward. She must have been in her mid-fifties and was quite large. Her husband was sitting next to her. I'd almost gone past her when I caught her glance, and her eyes were twinkling – she obviously wanted to play. I don't know what I did but I probably just produced my jar of Verysillin capsules, which are just long spring snakes that leap out of the jar when you take the lid off – two-foot springs covered in material to look vaguely like capsules! She started to laugh. But her husband started to cry. Then she started to cry, presumably because he was crying. I did something else and they both started to laugh together. It turned out that she had had a stroke three months previously and he'd started to cry because this was the first time she'd smiled, never mind laughed, since then. I was able to leave them with the hope of laughter and the possibility of happier and healthier times to come.

But rarely does the course of clowning run smoothly. In another ward I was having a great if raucous time with a couple of people in opposite beds, when I turned to the lady in the adjacent bed and only half-seriously apologized for all the noise. 'I should think so too!' she snapped back, for she wasn't in the least amused. You do have to be sensitive to everyone in any situation, and you have to be appropriate to them and their circumstances. Having said that, it's no good treating the hospital ward like a library and tiptoeing round ever so carefully, disturbing no one and just minding your own business – that's how everyone else behaves and that's not why I'm there.

There were a number of rejections and refusals through the week, which is inevitable, and a lot of the time I just felt terribly vulnerable, but there is no ministry without that side of it. I went into the Burns Unit on a particular invitation to see a young boy of about nine who had severe burns all over his body. He was surrounded by family when I put my head round the door, and he took one look me and and was pretty scornful. The family looked at me with even greater derision, as if to say, What have we got to laugh about? But I hung on for a while, and as I turned to leave the boy thanked me quite genuinely for coming to see him. Sometimes you just have to take the flak; it's what you're there for. The clown's fate and calling is to be the scapegoat. All ministry is carried out with a certain amount of trepidation. Nevertheless, a bit of creative anarchy and a lot of laughter remain exactly what the doctor ordered, even if clowns need both the will and the stamina to deliver them.

There were any number of brief encounters during that week. There was a doctor in orthopaedics who asked if he could be my apprentice. A sister in the maternity ward begged me not to come because they'd had enough births for one day and didn't want me to start the rest off! I obviously tickled the fancy of the lady in the Gynaecology Outpatients department who burst into peals of laughter at the sight of me appearing with my feather duster, shouting that she could have done with it five minutes before. A dour-faced auxiliary pushing a wheelchair remarked glumly to the man in his charge that I must be one of those clowns, he supposed. But increasingly through the week, there was a chorus of 'There's that clown again!', and it was usually said with appreciation, anticipation or delight. The transport manager said to me on the Friday that I'd made a lot of people happy that week, and if he was right, then I'd certainly done my job. If the hospital had become a bit more human and more humorous because of my antics, if I'd injected a bit of soul into the place, then I'd achieved all that I'd set out for and more. But when the clown's about, that's the sort of thing that happens.

When I was teaching clowning in the USA in the summer of 2000 I met Joe Barney, an extremely large and very funny clown who is one of Michael Christensen's colleagues. Joe is in charge of setting up Clown Care Units in hospitals around the States. His character is an absurdly absent-minded Professor of Fartiology, so absent-minded that he keeps forgetting to put his trousers on. He always has some farting putty in his pocket, and is a dab hand at producing noises of all kinds and volumes. He takes great delight in standing in a crowded lift, letting rip with a less than discreet noise, and then looking innocent as he watches everybody else pretend they hadn't heard it, never mind done it. Just as the doors open at the next floor, he turns to the most important-looking, pompous doctor in the lift, and says, 'Honestly. This is a hospital!', and walks out. It seems to me that as always it's very important to bring down the mighty from their seats and to lampoon authority. There are occasions when the clown needs to disperse some of that mystique that surrounds the medical profession. Doctors and nurses remain as human as we are and thus just as fallible, and they and we need reminding of that from time to time. It is also good in a hospital to play around with bodily functions. In a place where bodily functions of all descriptions are metered and measured and charted so often and so meticulously, the clown who farts at will is not only doing what clowns have always done, I think he's saying something about the place. Only the fool is foolish enough to be vulgar in the midst of so much hygiene and science! That doesn't mean that I will be farting my way round Odstock, but it does mean that Joe will keep doing what he does best, and will leave people in hysterics in the process.

If a hospital is to be a healthy place it must be able to laugh at itself. If its patients are to get better, they must be allowed to be themselves and laugh their way to wholeness and health. Who knows, it might even speed the journey. It may be too that the clown can help a person to a happy death. There's a memorable sequence in the Patch Adams film where Patch does exactly that, where a man who finds him, and everybody else, totally offensive to begin with, is brought to an acceptance of himself and his fate, and in the end dies peacefully. Death can't be judged as failure – it happens to the best of us! The clown is best equipped to play with failure and the idea of failure and show them up for the impostors they are. Each person in any hospital is an individual with individual needs, and needing to be treated as such. A person in bed shouldn't suddenly be treated as a case of whatever the illness happens to be – she's still Shirley or Mum or Gran. The doctor in his menacing white coat isn't just a doctor, he's Doctor Hopkins, with a wife and a sick child at home. Clowns take the time to call people by name and to listen too. They invite us to play, and somehow embody our hopes and our fears. We know they understand because they show us ourselves and help us to laugh, because of and despite everything. They'll share and provoke both laughter and tears, break the taboos of our imagination and making, and take us to places we never dared dream of. Now that's what I call patient care! Clowning with passion and compassion works wonders.

6

Clown and Story

One of my favourite stories is the old medieval tale of Our Lady's Juggler. There's a lovely version of it by Tomie de Paola, called *The Clown of God*, that I use from time to time. I was first introduced to it by Sandra Pollerman, that superb storyteller and clown, and then was given a copy by two great friends whose wedding I conducted. In those days the book was published by Methuen. Of course I've changed it in odd details but in substance the story remains the same. It's changed because it's become my story and in a way it tells my story, as all good stories should.

It's about a boy called Giovanni, who sees a troupe of clowns and decides that's what he wants to be – just as I did with going to the circus and seeing Coco and his troupe. He succeeds, of course, and travels miles, clowning and juggling. One day he has a meeting with a couple of Franciscan friars who assure him that all that he does sings to the glory of God – which I'm sure it does. But he pours scorn on the idea and condemns it all as religious rubbish. Towards the end of his life, his tricks start to go wrong, people begin to laugh at him instead of with him, and finally he decides it's time to go home and take off his clown face for ever. On his way back home, on a cold, cold night, he takes shelter in a huge abbey where he falls soundly asleep. He is woken by the sounds of lots of people who are all leaving gifts in front of a statue of Mary and the boy Jesus. He remembers it's Christmas Eve. He has nothing to offer, but after the rest have all gone he goes up to the statue and sees with alarm that the face of the boy Jesus is terribly solemn. He knows that he used to be able to make children laugh, so he does his act one last time, solely for the benefit of this statue of the boy Jesus. But the old clown falls dead on the floor at the climax of the act. In rush the verger and the abbot to find not only the body of the dead clown, but also that he has worked wonders, for the statue of the boy is smiling and in his hands he holds Giovanni's golden juggling ball. It is a story that I have always found moving and one that many others have too. There are occasions when there's hardly a dry eye in the house, and people from five to a hundred-and-five get caught up in it.

On one occasion I told the story in the hospice ward of Odstock Hospital. I had been ushered round the back to the communal sitting room because one of the cancer patients had just died. The mood was sombre, to say the least, but about ten other patients were gathered. We had chatted and played a bit, and then I told this story. I finished with a couple of silly gags. There were lots of tears and lots of laughter, and I was told afterwards that my presence and that story, with its mixture of laughter and tears, had at last enabled one of those listeners to come to terms with her terminal illness, as well as opening up several of the others. One man started to talk about his life as a circus lorry-driver, which came as a surprise to everyone. But stories provoke more stories which speak profoundly of ourselves. In story we connect with each other, and in the best stories we identify ourselves completely. The chaplain commented at the time that she had never seen them so attentive or so full of life, and how important it was to speak of death and to allow or provoke tears. In taking on the story of Giovanni's life and death, they were taking on their own story of life and death too, and perhaps for the first time they could see a smile on the face of God at having done so.

The power of story is immense. The best stories have an archetypal quality and are ultimately to do with self-revelation. When I went to Fool Time, the circus school, probably the hardest thing we had to do was halfway through our second term, when we were each asked to entertain all the others for just one minute. That sounds easy, really. There were twenty-two of us on the course, from all over Europe. We had all passed auditions to get there, and most of us had some professional or at least semi-professional experience. The school was a converted church hall, and all we had to do was come from one side to the middle and do our stuff. However, there's always a but, and this was a big but: if anyone in the audience got remotely bored even for a moment, they had to walk away. Good sermon training! I, like most of the others, failed miserably. Those of us who attempted to do something terribly clever, or who resorted to tried and trusted material, found their audience turning away in droves.

Some had gone even before the performer got to the middle – it teaches you a lot about how to make entrances and exits! The only two who managed it at all were two who in one way or another told their own story, who were brave enough and foolish enough to reveal something of themselves. They didn't deal in facts and figures and bio-graphical details, but they did reveal more important things such as their passion and their passions. Then we wanted to stay, to watch and to listen. Never mind all the fancy stuff – this was the stuff of life. It was a lesson I've held dear ever since. Never mind all the circus props and clown gags and spectacular stunts that I use in storytelling and performance, it's me that's the most important prop, resource and story.

It's back to the crucial figure and idea of the clown as jester, the truth-teller who can only speak of truth if he is himself truthful, and can only ultimately reveal truth if he is prepared to reveal himself in the process. If there is any fraud or falseness in me, I'm soon found out, and I lose not only credibility but my audience. Children know it in an instant. If I'm only pretending to be a clown, they'll soon tell me, and it won't matter how many times I tell them that I am really a clown, it won't help; but if I am truly a clown, they'll know it. If I tell them something that comes from the heart, they'll listen and engage; if I read them something that comes from a script or do something that isn't mine and which I haven't made my own, then I can't expect my audience to make it their own either. 'Clowning from the heart' has become the byword in the USA for good clowning or real clowning, and in this sense it is certainly true, for clowning from the heart connects – as long as it's not gushingly from the heart! Maybe clowning from the soul is a better description, for clowning from the soul suggests a profoundness that all clowns and storytellers must seek if they are not only to tell their story but discover it. Clowning from the soul speaks of spirituality as well as compassion, and suggests it comes from the depths.

But however heartfelt or soul-deep your clowning or your story, both benefit from good technique, so let's look briefly at some of those techniques. The voice is the most obvious tool when storytelling, and if that's flat or monotonous, then it doesn't matter how good the material is, it ain't gonna work. Voice needs variation in speed and tone and volume. And that means not using the voice too – taking good pauses, dwelling in the silence when that's appropriate, and breaking it again at just the right time. It's too easy to be frightened of the silence but it's then that some of the profound things happen. It's also natural to speed everything up – I do if I'm nervous, so I have to catch myself doing it when that happens and just slow down.

It's not just the voice, it's the body too. People talk a lot these days about body language – television commentators do about sportsmen especially! But the body does have a language of its own and we have to use it. Gestures are important as long as we don't overdo them – it's just as important not to mumble movement as it is not to mumble words. Gestures aren't just hand and arm movements, it's head and knee and hips and all sorts! And the body must reflect the mood of the story too – taut in suspense, deflated in disappointment, light in rejoicing, heavy in sadness, and so on. When I went to one of his workshops, Kenny Ahern, a brilliant American silent clown, put into words what I do naturally, for his constant chorus was 'angles and levels'. If your body stays upright all the time, if your arms stay down by your sides, if there's no movement and energy and nothing is happening physically, then nothing much is going to happen anywhere else either. But once you start moving and bending and crooking elbows and reaching to the floor and cocking your head to one side, then things start to happen. What I really aim to do is to live the story, to be the story, to make it happen. If I live it, I stop it being second-hand. In re-enacting the story I bring it back to life. I become Giovanni in order that people can see not me but Giovanni, and watch him unobserved. And then through my eyes and Giovanni's eyes, they might see the statue of the Christ child themselves.

To do that, I have to establish and then maintain eye

contact with the audience. It's no good talking to the floor or addressing the ceiling – they don't want to hear my story. It's amazing how many preachers in pulpits reserve their very deepest theological insights for the ceiling's enjoyment and benefit! Meet the audience eye to eye, face to face. It's the only way to connect, to contact. We equate looking people in the eye with being truthful and honest and straight with them. This is exactly the same, for here stands the truth-teller, being straight and truthful, and he has nothing to hide. He only wants us to look him in the eye and see.

The secret of storytelling is not that you make them listen to what you want them to hear, but that you help them see for themselves. In that way they enter into the story and it becomes their own because they are in it too. I always tell my Christmas story as an introduction to a show, and I tell it as if I were jester to one of the three kings and had gone on ahead because they were far too busy gossiping and gazing at the stars. I therefore get to Bethlehem just in time for the birth, and the battered old box that I've been balancing on on top of a log becomes the bed in which the baby Jesus is then laid. Many children through the years have asked me if I was really there, to which the answer is, of course, yes, because in some sense we all were. But the art has been in taking those children into the stable in Bethlehem in order for them to see the baby Jesus for themselves. And in that kind of seeing comes believing. The storyteller has to see it for himself in order to allow others to see it too.

Storytelling thus becomes a matter of description rather than prescription, for we describe what we see. It needs those splashes of colour and pertinent detail and the snatches of mood and dialogue, but the bulk is left for the listeners or watchers to fill in individually. The best stories speak for themselves. Some of the very best stories are biblical ones, but churches have a tendency to kill them stone dead before they even start. A lesson is read rather than the story told, and in many places we're told beforehand what's going to happen, what it means, what the context is, and, horror of horrors, the page number in the Bible so that we don't need to listen at all. Surely we can read the Word of God at home but listen to it proclaimed in church! But oh no, we'd rather reduce the Word to words, in fact as many words as possible. If I tell my audience what they're going to hear before they hear it, I rob the story of all suspense and any surprise – and both are necessary to good stories. The gospel is supposed to be Good News, not yesterday's news. If I remind them that they've heard this one before, they'll switch off – oh no, not the Good Samaritan again! But if I as storyteller tell the story of the Good Samaritan as if I've never heard it before, then it's going to be different. Indeed if I can tell it in such a way as I might do if I've dashed home and am recounting the story as I've just heard it from the lips of Jesus himself, then it's going to be different – and it's going to be received differently. This art of telling the story as if for the first time brings a freshness and a new dimension, and allows listeners to see things in a new light and be affected by odd bits and details that might not have struck them before.

If we throw humour into the cocktail, as all clowns should, then we get an even headier brew. Let's laugh at the priest walking snootily by on the other side, chuckle as the Samaritan tries to heave the injured and grossly overweight victim on to the ancient creaky donkey, and giggle at the drunks falling over their own feet as they stagger out of the inn. Humour makes us look at it differently. For the clown nothing and everything is sacred. So the truth is told, but it doesn't mean that every verse from scripture is sacred. We can leave verses out, throw in ridiculous scenes, give the anonymous characters improbable names – we can do what we like, so long as there remains a reverence for the truth and the opportunity for revelation. If the humour is genuine, it will work because humour and truth go hand in hand. People have to be given the time and the space to get the joke, to see it for themselves, and to be surprised by it.

The best punchlines are always surprising, and we need to rediscover the gospel punchlines and then learn how to deliver them. The model we have from Jesus is to use parables and punchlines. He used lots of stories and even more punchlines. It's the punchlines that people remember – be they from Jesus, Groucho Marx, Oscar Wilde, W. C. Fields or Tommy Cooper! Punchlines surprise us, but they also encapsulate both the story and the point of the story, and thus act as cue cards when we want to recall them. Punchlines don't have to make us fall about with laughter, they can seem to be a bit below the belt, they can take the wind out of us. They are extremely effective. Jesus told stories because he knew that was the best way, and if sometimes he had to explain what on earth he was on about to his rather dim-witted disciples, then so be it. But he didn't explain the deeper meaning to all his listeners – they were left to draw their own conclusions. One of the beauties of both clowning and storytelling is that they work on so many different levels. A story can be taken at face value or it can lead us right down below the surface to another place. Those that have ears hear, and those that have eyes see, and yet the same story can mean totally different things to different people.

One of the things I have discovered over the years is that in the telling you discover not only the punchlines but the story itself. I might work out a script beforehand, and

I always try to visualize it all as I'm doing it, and then I learn it as best I can. Come the first performance, the script is left firmly in the vestry or wherever and I just have to do it. And it's then that things start to happen! I discover new lines and better lines, partly because of the physical demands of doing it, the things that I find myself doing. It is also because suddenly I'm bouncing off an audience, and the audience will always feed me lines and ideas. And it is because in the end I discover the rhythm of the story and also the proper rhythm of the sentences and the punchlines. I do a story about Adam and the Fall with the help of a rolling globe which I balance on, and it changed an awful lot over the first six or eight times of telling. The final punchline was a classic example of finding the rhythm. I used to say, 'I'd much rather be loved by God than like him.' I knew it wasn't quite right because it suggested I didn't really want to like him! As soon as the time came when I said, 'I'd much rather be loved by God than be like him,' I knew I had it at last. In fact, in my Old Testament video, *Only Fools and Heroes*, we still had the original line when I recorded it in a local orchard, but fortunately I discovered the real line before the video was finally produced and the editor was able to dub in the extra 'be'! The wonders of technology!

The Giovanni story has developed its own choreography, its proper movement. A bonus of this is that I don't need to remember the words because the body keeps giving me the cues throughout. It's a godsend for the times when I've just been distracted or interrupted by a small child or some such, because I know where I am in the story by the position I'm in! The more I know my story, the more I live it, and the better I connect with my audience because I don't have to think about the words. I don't want the words to get in the way. The physical telling of the story accentuates the rhythm of the story as well as underlines some of its salient points. The Adam story is the same. It revolves around the rolling globe, so I stand on it, sit on it, juggle on it, hide behind it, roll over it and so on and never really let go of it, and thus there's a natural flow to both the movement and the story as well as a focus for it all. If I go with the flow, then my audience will be able to as well. The more hiccups we can get rid of by discovering the natural rhythms, the less opportunity the audience has to be distracted or jolted out of the story and back into the so-called real world of shopping, work and local gossip. In the story we want to try and take them out of all that, and not give them a chance to leap back into its cosy familiarity until the story is over, indeed until the whole experience is complete.

One of the best ways that I've found to take people into the story is simply to take them with me. That means, of course, that I have to be in the story as well. The clown has the capacity to step into the shoes of any character and become him or her. This chameleon-like quality is largely due to the mystical nature of the clown. The clown is timeless and seems to live outside and beyond the limits of our ordinary mortal lives. I can have been in the stable at Bethlehem or in the temple at Jerusalem or by the banks of the Red Sea, and nobody wonders how or why. As long as I believe it, you can. Communication is by conviction. So I can become St Peter or Judas or Noah or Jonah or Moses in an instant, because the clown can just conjure them up and off we go. If I don't quite believe it, if I approach it with that implicit attitude that suggests that of course I'm not really St Peter but please could you go along with it, then it isn't going to work. You can't be apologetic. You have to go for it! If you really go for it, we'll all come with you.

One of the ways of helping people come with me is to start with the ordinary and familiar and then lead them up the garden path to somewhere that is certainly extraordinary and sometimes quite unnerving. My story of Judas does that, almost literally! It's all based on kisses, and in fact it was first devised when I led a youth weekend down in Fawley, and the Sunday service was on St Valentine's Day. It's changed a lot since then, not least because I don't have the regular use of a dozen teenage clowns dashing on and kissing each other ridiculously! I start by blowing up what turns out to be an inflatable heart printed with the immortal words 'I love you'. Then taking a flower from a vase I coyly present it to a woman in the audience and blow her a kiss, hoping to get one in return. Usually I get one in the end, but it doesn't matter if I don't because I dash back and get another flower. This one is a bit bigger and grander, and I find another woman in the audience and again hope for a response, implicitly an even bigger and more ready response! Last but not least, I dash back and produce a ludicrously large weed, and cast my eye eagerly over the audience. The weed has already been broken in two somewhere towards the bottom, and I hold it over the break – it's an old clown gag. I present my trophy to a lady who is obviously enjoying all the nonsense, she grasps it at the bottom, and I turn away still carrying the major part of the weed, leaving her with a solitary stalk. I turn again and apologize profusely, and blow one more kiss. It's a good laugh when it works and if it has worked, they're with me already and comfortable in silly nonsense. I then admit that I hate kisses because I find kissing so embarrassing. – which I do really, in terms of greeting people at the door and kissing them politely and all that sort of thing. Then I ask if they remember their first real kiss, and it's always obvious on a number of faces that some of them do. In my mind I remember the first time I kissed Jane, my wife, which remains a very special moment in my life. There are always a few smiles and nervous giggles, especially from the younger end of the audience. I go on to say that I remember mine, that I can still feel the tingle in my spine when it happened – and I often can! – and that I was floating on air, which I was! But that I soon came down to earth. I confess then that it all happened in the garden and that I only did it to identify him, which was so silly because they knew who he was. I was such a fool because it wasn't until I kissed him that I knew how much I loved him ... Suddenly we're in the Garden of Gethsemane as the soldiers drag him away and the Christ is crucified for a kiss. And if I have managed to get there into the garden, then most of the congregation will be peering over my shoulder and witnessing it for themselves. That's the power of story. That's the kind of style I have developed. The clown in all his foolishness leads us on, and he leads us on to an understanding of the foolishness of God that is much wiser than our wisdom.

Circus, Story and Slapstick has become my slogan because I use clown gags and old clown routines and circus skills, and all the mess and nonsense and the courage and bravado all that involves, to tell not just the story of God but also my story and my pilgrimage, which is really the only way into that more important story, the story I actually want to tell. In the Judas story, parts of me inform it and an old clown gag introduces it, and we see not just the comedy of the clown but also his tragic dimension. I am convinced that if a clown is going to preach the gospel, he or she must do so as only a clown would and could. It's no good doing a magic trick and then getting serious, or doing a clown routine and then stepping out of character and out of the moment to explain exactly why you did what you did and what your audience are supposed to take from it. I'm afraid I don't have a lot of time for terribly clever little tricks that are then explained stage by stage and their Christian relevance spelt out to a bewildered and obviously theologically dyslexic congregation. I'd rather deal in symbols than visual aids because symbols have power and different levels of meaning. A symbol's not really a symbol if I have to explain it or, worse still, put a written sign underneath it like a museum exhibit. In the same way, I have to leave the story or gag to fend for itself, and I have to do it my way – not just the clown's way but my clown's way. Instead of relying on cold reason and seasoned argument, I have to hope that amidst the laughter and the tears and the mayhem, the truth has been revealed in ways that I need know nothing about and certainly have no control over. The clown isn't the spoonful of sugar to help the medicine go down, he has his own medicine in his hands but, clown that he is, he has no idea what it's for, where it's been taken, and how often. He does, however, suspect that it can be taken by anyone for anything at any time and in any place. His job is simply to play the spoons!

It seems an anomaly to me for a clown to preach a straight sermon, and I certainly try to avoid that. I think I have been forced into that position only a couple of times in the last ten years and both went all right, but clowning would have been better because doing it is always better than talking about it. It's also because people actually have to know what you're talking about by experiencing it, and experience is much better than hearsay. I was able in preaching to tell a bit of my story and talk about the what and the why and the how, and I guess that's interesting, otherwise you wouldn't be reading this book! But the clown's story is much more powerful than the story of a man who is dressed as a clown talking about being one. Seeing what the clown is and does is infinitely preferable to hearing about it. It's back to the basic rule of thumb that if you can do it without a red nose on, then do it without that red nose. I can preach a sermon without a red nose on, perfectly capably. With a red nose on, it has to be different.

Back in 1993 or 1994, I was asked by the Board of Mission and Social Responsibility in Southwark Diocese to do something for them in their annual service. It was to be in Southwark Cathedral, the preacher was Archbishop Trevor Huddleston, and it was on the Feast of Candlemas, so the gospel for the day, and thus my subject matter, was the story of Simeon in the Temple prophesying over the baby Jesus that here basically was the Messiah. I read the story and re-read it, and then began to picture the scene and to think of different possibilities.

The key for me lay in the words of the actual prophecy that 'this child is destined for the fall and the rising of many, destined to be a sign that is rejected so that the secret thoughts of many may be laid bare.' I suddenly thought of using a diabolo, which soars up in the air and down again when thrown. Simeon suddenly became this mad and much-mocked veteran figure of fun who had stood by the temple door as long as anyone could remember, as if he was waiting for something to happen or someone to come. He'd always played with his diabolo, tossing it up and down, much to the amusement of the children, who teased him mercilessly. Come the moment when the Christ child is brought to the temple for the rites of purification, it is that absurd and battered old diabolo that serves him in his prophecy – and it is a prophecy that none would forget. Well, the story all came together. I hurried off to buy a diabolo, learned the rudiments of it in about twenty minutes – I had to, I was doing it the next day! – and the story took shape. I mentioned in an earlier chapter about him saying that he had to keep his whiphand over the devil so that he knows who is its master, and there are images like that that add greatly to the sense and semblance of the story.

I began with my old favourite silly trick of tearing up a newspaper into lots of little pieces in the failed attempt to make it disappear, only to console myself with the assurance that 'Blessed are the piecemakers'. It was great to get those worthy supporters of the Board of Mission and Social Responsibility, a body of people not renowned for playfulness and humour, all to shout out three magic words to try and make it work! I became a witness to it all rather than Simeon himself, and yet I represented Simeon too as I tossed the diabolo up in the air and to my relief caught it again. Then I tossed it away as I warned that the sign would be rejected. In the end Simeon is shooed out of the temple and told never to come back again, and the Christ child is handed to me. I concluded that I didn't know why he was handed to me unless somehow Mary knew that I would live not just to tell the tale of the birth of the Prince of Peace but also of his proclamation, and that maybe we might be foolish enough to join with him, the Prince of Peace, and one day ourselves become peacemakers. The final image was again of scraps of newspaper showering over my head, and as I turned my final rejoinder was the disillusioned observation that that had been a long time ago and still there was no peace. Trevor Huddleston enjoyed it and was moved by it, apparently. This was before the dismantling of apartheid in South Africa, the country he loved so much and had served so well, but afterwards he said to the Provost of the Cathedral that he wanted that clown at the service on the day that South Africa became a free country. I was honoured at the thought and by the accolade, though of course it never happened – me being at the service, that is! But Trevor Huddleston was a great man, and all the greater for the playful twinkle in his eye.

For many that evening, Southwark Cathedral had become for a while the old temple at Jerusalem and here was the clown as prophet himself using circus skills, story and slapstick to speak of the things of God and the demands of God. The diabolo was intrinsic to the story, not an optional extra or a bit of skill just to capture attention, a sprat to catch a mackerel. The story had been about an old man whom everybody thought was quite mad yet who turned out to be no fool but rather the wisest person I had ever met. The proper way to understand him, of course, is to know that it is precisely because he is a fool that he has such wisdom, but most of my stories have an element of that. Who but a fool would build an ark in his front garden? Who but a fool could be coughed up by a whale and land up by the seaside? Who but a fool could believe that she was pregnant by the Holy Spirit? And who but the fool of her husband would believe her? The heroes of faith are an extremely foolish lot, on the whole! Yet we are called to follow their example and not just believe but enter their story.

Some of the saints are just as bad – or good, depending on your viewpoint. Most people allow that the greatest saints have also at some time been the greatest sinners. But it's also true that some of the saints have also been the greatest jokers. St Francis of Assisi's followers were known as his *joculatores*, his merrymakers or jokers, and laughter was said to resound in the highways and byways, wherever they went. St Teresa of Avila has that wonderful prayer that would fit in any litany: 'From silly devotions and sour-faced saints, Good Lord deliver us'! I would canonize Eric Morecambe immediately if I were Pope!

But it's great fun playing with the stories of the saints too. In 1997, I was asked to do something for the fourteen-hundredth anniversary of St Augustine's arrival in Britain – in fact for all three days of the celebrations, but on the Friday evening I had to do something in Canterbury Cathedral. Because of the numbers expected as well as the poor sight lines in terms of possible performance, it was agreed I would do something from the pulpit. Not a sermon – the Archbishop was doing that. I think my contribution was billed as a comment! I told the story of Augustine as if I had been his jester, and admitted that my task had always been to try and make St Augustine less august and more auguste, in other words to stop him taking himself so seriously. I spent some of the story with an enormous floral, tasselled lampshade on my head, which I had always worn in procession behind Gus (he hadn't been a saint in those days!) in order to remind him not to believe his own publicity. He had been known by the populace as the Herald of the Light of Christ, for he was credited with making Britain a Christian country, but it was after all the light of Christ not the light of Gus. I sometimes called him the Great Gusto because he was such an enthusiast, and it did put him in his place! It was all a bit wordy but it was fun. I even suggested that Gus would have been chuffed to have known that he'd had a roundabout in Canterbury named after him, and that St Augustine's Roundabout wasn't a bad nickname for the Church of England!

St Alban got much the same treatment when St Alban's Abbey wanted me to come and celebrate their Rose Day. The day commemorates the martyrdom of St Alban, the first English martyr, and specifically the story that the hill where he died, next to where the Abbey now stands, suddenly blossomed with flowers. That's a wonderful story for a holy fool, if ever there was one, and I played it to the full. The plot involved costume changes – St Alban swapped clothes with a Christian who was being hunted down by the authorities – so we were away. St Alban became Alby, which was as much an affectionate tribute to Alby Austin, one of the famous Austin clown dynasty of this country, as a nickname for a saint. I used the story several times, unlike the Gus one which was a one-off for a special occasion. But I guess it would have found a better form and rhythm with a bit more mileage. Nevertheless, this timeless jester figure is a multi-purpose character when it comes to telling stories. I'm very lucky, for here is an incredible and yet totally credible character who can get away with murder whilst speaking of the things of faith with the voice and experience of firsthand witness. Only a fool would attempt it!

But the clown is himself story. He somehow contains all our stories and reflects them. For ten years Steve Smith was the Principal of Clown College in the USA and thus heavily involved in the training of many of the clowns working in America today. His brief was to produce the best possible clowns for the so-called and self-styled Greatest Show on Earth, in other words, the Ringling Brothers and Barnum & Bailey Circus. He maintains that definition at least in terms of role, for he sees the clown as Everyman who holds up the funhouse mirror to life and to all our stories. All that the clown does has to have basic truth at its core, so that however ridiculous the clown's actions, both the truth and the story are discernible. His job was largely to ensure the clarity of thought and process that made the story followable. There has to be a beginning, a middle and an end, and a point to it all – a punchline or blow-off, as they call it. Whereas he admits that all performers are storytellers in some sense, using the arts to tell that story, clowns are the most accessible because they grant us permission to feel true feelings, to get in touch with ourselves and to connect with the story. Whatever kind of clowning anyone does, a clown's task is to touch hearts. One way to do that is simply to be the story. If we move one step sideways away from the Greatest Show on Earth and into the Greatest Story Ever Told, if we allow that description or definition of the Bible, then the clown's job is still to be the story because it's the most valid way of making the Word of God incarnate. That's surely what the whole gospel demands of us – not to talk about it but to be it, not just to tell the story but to be the story.

Maybe we can't all be the story quite yet, but I think we're all storytellers, if we give ourselves permission. We've all got as many stories inside us as we've had moments in our lives. We just need to draw them out and test and taste them. If we let them out, they'll begin to find their finished and polished form, and might just help establish and maintain the rhythm of our lives. Of course, most of us haven't the courage or the vision to do that – just as back at Fool Time most of us made do with the familiar or the fancy stuff, ever hoping to impress. But some of us will dare to reveal something of ourselves in the story, and if some of us do tell, it might just encourage others to tell their story too.

7

Prayer and Playfulness

A recurring theme of this book, and indeed my constant invitation and chorus, is simply, 'Let us play'. It is what clowns do – we play. We play with ideas and situations and see what we can make from them. We play with people who want to play with us, and encourage those who don't want to play not to be such spoilsports and to join in. We play with words and thus make outrageous puns. We play with institutions and traditions and authorities to test their relevance and authenticity. We play with status and the status quo. And I play endlessly in church! It's what churches are for. They are houses of prayer but they are also places to play, to take leisure, to simply let go.

Churches are designed to be different. Built to the glory of God (but let's not forget the architect!), they are set apart. They are set apart in terms of function because the things that go on inside churches are distinctly different from what goes on outside them – or they should be. And they are set apart in terms of design and size and structure. They are always quite distinctive – you can spot a church a mile off, but then you're supposed to be able to. This is certainly true of the older churches in Britain, but it is also true of most of the new ones, and I think the same applies the world over. It is a great shame that in Britain today so many churches are kept firmly locked throughout the week for fear of vandals, thieves and arsonists. It defeats the purpose of the buildings being there, which is to provide a haven away from the busy everyday world for people to come to for rest, refreshment and prayer. The church should be a place that has nothing to do with work, that presents no stress, and which embodies the possibilities inherent in the Kingdom of God. That to me is a place of play, a place to take your ease, a place where different rules apply and all things are possible.

Churches are so wonderfully impractical! Impossible to heat, they rise grandly above the neighbouring buildings to such an extent that it's a major exercise even to change a light bulb! But that's half the glory. There is no need for churches to be utilitarian in design or purpose. Thanks to the invention of pews, many churches are totally useless for anything that doesn't involve people sitting in serried ranks facing forward. But churches celebrate the value of uselessness and the wisdom of folly. There's something about all these strange buildings that speaks of the foolishness of God. There are what are called architectural follies dotted around Britain's landscapes, and these take the form of tall turrets and towers and the like, all built to satisfy the whim of some eccentric with far more money than sense, not to mention taste. Church buildings can't be accused of being totally useless in the way that follies are, but they have more than a few similarities. There is a sense in which church buildings in all their grandeur and solidity speak of this eccentric God, with far more love than sense, who wants to provide places which are not built just for his own private pleasure or there just to be admired by passers-by, but which are spaces where people can gather to play together.

It's the silly bits in church architecture that I like most. I love the gargoyles on the drainpipes, and the daft faces on roof bosses. I marvel at the intricacy of some of the carpenters' and masons' work, with all their frilly bits. I wonder at the vision demanded to build such places on such a scale. But I guess what impresses me most are the misericords, those carved heads and faces and sculptures that are underneath the seats in the choirs of cathedrals and abbeys throughout the land. Here was the chance to leave your mark, to have the last laugh, and yet spend infinite care in getting it just right, even though it would only be on very rare occasions that anyone would see the fruit of your labours. The time and motion experts of today wouldn't allow any such nonsense, that's for sure; but our churches, thank God, are full of nonsense, and long may they remain so! Yes, let us play!

I suppose it depends on what you think God is like as to whether you agree with all this nonsense! Earlier on I've suggested that God is the God of laughter and of tears, who laughs with us and cries with us. Surely God is the playful God, but not in the sense of the Tess of the d'Urbervilles or Moby Dick vision of God, who just plays with us as a plaything to be discarded at will. God is a God of love, God the Father, who delights in his sons and his daughters, and plays with them as all loving parents do. Of course, if he wasn't the father, he'd have rather less interest in us – there's nothing worse than babytalk to those who aren't the actual parents! But since he is God the Father he cares, and plays endlessly, going to such foolish lengths that an outsider finds it all quite incredible. But God's love is the love that is laughter. It isn't a possessive, distorted, judgmental love, but rather a love that is open, constant and free, a love that wills the best for his children but cannot dictate their present never mind their future, a love which continues to play in the moment, regardless of the past and yet promising a future. The first thing God does once he has created man is to create a playmate for him, for the Garden of Eden is such paradise because all they have to do is play together. Love as well as greed and ambition complicates it all, and work is the curse and punishment for all parties. But we were made to play. God the Creator must have a wondrous sense of humour not just to have created all those ridiculous creatures of the earth in all their shapes and sizes and with all their ludicrous noises, but also to have created us with all our weaknesses and foibles and irresistible temptations. But the world of play is a world of grazed knees and great adventures and someone always wanting to be King of the Castle. It is of what we are made. But God's reassurance is that it won't always end in tears. Like all good clowns, we pick ourselves up, dust ourselves down, and start all over again. It's the laughter of heaven that makes it all possible.

Once we begin to see the church building as the playroom of the living, laughing God, it does rather change our perception of what's appropriate or what's inappropriate in church. It doesn't mean that everything's got to be awfully jolly – that really would be terrible! There are enough places already with that sickening 'Smile – God loves you' mentality. Some games are very solemn and splendid and rather theatrical, others are simple and straightforward. Some games demand great concentration, others are a breeze and just good for a laugh. Some of the things in the toybox may seem quite alien to begin with, but they soon become familiar friends. Other things in the toybox are things that we really have always wanted, and we find that we're not disappointed. Sometimes a new game might be introduced, and that's difficult when you've got favourite games that seem quite satisfactory, but new games always have something to offer and sometimes they supplant the old games only too quickly and almost seamlessly. Some playrooms are huge and light and airy and full of pictures and primary colours, while others are small and cosy and comforting. We can of course dress up in the playroom, or choose to come as we are and dress down. You can choose to play on your own, but it never lasts long and you find it's much more fun joining in. Especially when you've learnt the rules!

All games have rules, even if they are few. Even if we make the game up as we go along, we make rules along the way. We need shape and structure. We need limits and boundaries, though we may choose either to extend them or reduce them once we've started to play the game. It's very difficult for most of us to join in wholeheartedly if we have no idea what we're doing or what's expected of us. If the rules are too complicated, we tend to give up and move on. Rules must be logical, fair, and make sense, but they just provide the framework for the fun and can never be the be-all and end-all.

I hope that the analogies of what goes on in our churches and amongst our congregations are fairly obvious. Let me just add that I think there are too many churches with too many rules, both rules about worship and rules about how to live our lives. It's the whiteface mentality that increases ten commandments to six hundred and ten in the pursuit of controlling every last jot and tittle, while conveniently forgetting that Jesus reduced ten commandments to two: love God and love your neighbour. It seems pretty obvious to me that if we get those two right, everything else falls into place. Fool that I am, I'd rather trust people to get on with playing the game, once those two rules are in place. It's what St Augustine said: Love God, and do what you like. He didn't mean we had *carte blanche* to indulge in anything and everything. He means that if we get the God bit right, if we actually do love God and have a living relationship with him, then there's every chance that the things we do will be exactly the things God wants us to do – by default then, we can do what we like in the hope if not knowledge that we are doing his will. Yes, let's have guidance, but rules should be a help not a hindrance to both faith and worship.

It's the churches with too many rules who find me a threat! Enter the clown and the rulebooks go out of the window! Mind you, it's best to open the window first, for it is rules and not windows that are made to be broken! As a general rule, it's not advisable to offer me all six books required for the service as soon as I come in – or even at all! It's much more fun to play with a service sheet, and it's much more simple too. We keep coming back to KISS, Keep It Simple Stupid, the clown's mnemonic. As in performance, so in worship – the less we have to worry about the words and about whether these are the right ones and whether we're in the right place in the right book, the more chance we actually have of communing with God, which is after all why we've come in the first place. I go to some churches and find people in the congregation look-ing so smug because they always know where they are in the service that it would be tempting to wheel in a row of judges, just as in gymnastics or ice-skating, to hold up a row of perfect sixes and applaud! It must make God laugh. Sadly, they wouldn't hear his laughter because they're too concerned with themselves and their performance, too self-conscious to be conscious of the playful God.

Prayer that is playful doesn't let ourselves get in the way. Prayer that is playful takes off, it soars and leaps and ducks and dives, it's not grounded by dull custom or naked self-interest. Prayer that is playful is eager to get on with it, if only to see what might happen next. It doesn't matter if you've got the same service every week with the same words of the same prayers, because it's not the words that matter. Whatever the structure of a service, it's the praying and playing that counts. Don't just say prayers, play them. Play with them, play with their possibilities, and you discover the God who plays with us in the process.

One of the defining characteristics of the Holy Spirit is that childish playfulness which means he can never be found in the same place that you thought you'd left him. Elusive and full of mischief, he loves playing tag in the playground, happy to chase or be chased, always happy to be caught eventually because it gives him a swift go at catching someone else, and then he's off again once more. Uncontrollable and quite delightful, grown-ups watch and admire from a distance until the Spirit breaks the rules and tags them, and then they have to join in! Some refuse but that's inevitable because not everybody wants to play the game. But the game goes on ... and on ... and on! The Spirit is always there waiting for us to come back and play some more. He knows we'll come back. It's just a matter of time. Prayer that is playful keeps coming back for more.

I love going to church, especially as clown. I'm lucky because I'm invited to lots of very lively and some very holy places, and I suppose that any church that invites me must have not only the courage to take the risk but also the imagination to do so. Risk and courage and a sense of adventure alongside a vivid imagination are basic stuff for the playroom. They ought to be basic for worship too. I suppose the alternative is Monopoly yet again! I go to churches with all shades of churchmanship and am quite at ease in all of them – they're all the same really! And in most of those churches, at least on the days that I'm there, we end up with that whiff of playfulness in the air. In some of them, we're up and running from the start; some of them are slow starters, but we usually get there in the end. Oh yes, let us play!

It is a worry to some people. At a church in Hereford-shire, the husband of the Vicar came up to me after the service, at which I'd done my slackrope and all sorts of things, and told me he had great reservations about it all. I was just preparing to explain the theology and the logic, and talk about the Fool and so on, when he said how wonderful he thought it had all been but that he was worried because he didn't know what they were going to do the following week. That's said quite often by way of a joke as someone says to the vicar or minister, 'Follow that!', and everyone laughs. But this guy was serious. I think he really thought I shouldn't have come. His was a counsel of mediocrity: let's keep it safe, dull but safe; let's keep it the same.

Yet one of the joys of the Christian calendar is that there are high days and holy days. Christmas and Easter are the high points and we can all go barmy. When I was a vicar in Tooting I used to buy champagne for the congregation to drink at the back of the church on Easter Day morning – well, sparkling white wine anyway! It was, of course, sherry on Christmas morning but I got the church council to pay for that! Yet in the Anglican Church it's those days that make the trudging through the foothills of Trinity/Pentecost 1–100 worthwhile! Feast and fast, laughter and tears, heights and depths. There's no way that I could clown at the same church all the time because we can't feast every week. It's not going to be absolutely fantastic every time we go out to play. But equally we shouldn't reduce worship to fasting every week. We're supposed to celebrate the Eucharist and we need to celebrate it like a birthday from time to time. Clowns are good for birthday parties! The temptation is to be terribly adult and forget birthdays as we get older so that every day remains the same – and that brings us back to Herefordshire. My hope is that that church isn't quite the same any more. I hope that just as stories lead to more stories from other people, so my playfulness leads to more playfulness from other people. The Diocese of Ely had a lay conference in March 2001 and they called it a Lay Odyssey. I was there for the whole weekend and they definitely got more playful as the weekend went on. Once people have been given permission to play, it's very difficult to stop them!

Actually, I'm amazed anyone ever invites me at all. I do get up to all sorts of things. It varies from place to place because I have to judge how far I can go. I normally make sure that I'm around and visible for five minutes before the service actually starts, then. I creep on or wander in unannounced and start dusting round the altar and the rails and anywhere else that seems appropriate. If there are huge floral arrangements, I always dust them, just to upset the flower ladies! I often manage to blow out one of the candles by mistake and have some fun and games trying to relight it. I'm likely to play peek-a-boo with the kids, either from the pulpit or from behind the choirscreen or its equivalent. I might change the number of one of the hymns on the board. In one church I did that with everyone watching and it got the usual mixture of gasps and giggles, but by the time we got to the hymn they'd all forgotten I'd changed it. Nevertheless, like all good Anglicans making the best of a bad job, they valiantly started to try and sing the words of the wrong hymn to the tune being played! I stopped them and we started again. All that I do is done gently, with a mixture of blissful ignorance and blatant mischief, and it gets the congregation used to the idea that I'm there and that things might be a bit different this week. It also establishes that I'm not going to be loud and vulgar and soak them with water or be there just for the kids, and that I'm not going to encroach on their space, merely invite them into mine.

If the minister in charge of the service then comes and gives out the notices, he's likely to get dusted too. If he goes on too long and notices are often interminable – I'll yawn hugely, point to my watch or just slip listlessly to the floor and start snoring. If the Vicar then publishes the banns of marriage and asks if anyone present knows any reason in law why this couple may not be joined together in matrimony, up I leap, arm aloft, and march towards him – it's every vicar's nightmare that one day someone will raise an objection! It's always better if someone other than me presides at the service because it allows me to bounce off him as my whiteface figure of authority. If there's a procession, I'll lead him in with my feather duster, which establishes our relationship once and for all. A middle-aged man in Leek thought my clowning throughout the service had all been wonderful except for my leading in the vicar, which he had found offensive. The vicar hadn't, but he had!

Once in church I sometimes take the seat that's been assigned to me but only if it's a more formal church and it seems right to conform. More likely, I'll perch on the pulpit step or just sit on the floor if I have to. It's much better to loiter on the edges, to seem not quite to belong. In the hymns my feather duster becomes in turn a guitar, violin, clarinet or trombone. My song sheet seems to have a life of its own and may end up in several pieces. If there's a procession of uniformed organizations' flags or just the people who have taken the collection, they may suddenly find me in the lead or I'll salute them as they go past. It really doesn't matter what is happening, I have to remain in character and never switch off. I just have to react appro-

priately. That also means that during the confession
during the eucharistic prayer in a communion service
will simply focus on what's happening and avoid being
distraction. You can't upstage the sacraments! We need
the stillness amidst the mayhem, the calm after the storm.
Sometimes I'm asked to preside over communion too, and
I find that quite special because I don't do it very often. It
not only confirms my ministry as clown priest but it also in
some way says something about the clown's transforming
touch, so that once again the bread and wine become
Christ's body and blood.

As a rule of thumb, I tend to fit into whatever the usual
framework of service the church normally is. That way it's
recognizably the same the next time people come, if they've
not been before, as well as being recognizably the same
for the regulars, so that they can cling on to the familiar
wreckage! So I'll do stories or bits of nonsense in place of
the readings, and the slackrope for the sermon. I might do
the prayers with my bubbles. Those are the set pieces but
all the other playful bits can be just as important.

On occasions I might go up and receive the collection
bags, only to dash off with them in best burglar fashion.
I always bring them back, though! Or I might grab the
large brass plate it's all been piled on and balance the whole
lot on a stick as a way of offering up the gifts. When
Lichfield Diocese celebrated a major anniversary with 'The
Feast' back in 1997, I think, it was on a showground, so
naturally it poured with rain all day. The main service in
the afternoon was thus moved under cover. In the middle
of the service, after the collection had been brought up in
plastic buckets, the Bishop said to those whom the buckets
hadn't reached that there would be opportunity for them
to contribute after the service. Hearing that, I grabbed one
of the buckets and thrust it in front of him. The Bishop

laughed and duly dug out his wallet from beneath all his robes, and in went a ten pound note. The congregation all laughed and applauded as all the other dignitaries on stage then had to follow suit!

The joy and secret of playfulness lie in the seizing of the moment rather than the seizing of a bucket, but the world of prayer is the same as the world of play, for both depend on that seizing of the moment. The world of play and prayer is a realm where we are suddenly allowed to see things differently, and to see them from a different perspective; a realm where all things are indeed possible, for it is a world of miracle and truth; a realm that demands our involvement as well as our imagination. Prayer at its most momentous is purely to be revelled in, for then we are immersed in the love and purposes of God. It's fun to splash around in the shallows, but in the end we need to venture past our tiptoes towards the deep end. The great discovery is finding that with God you are never out of your depth. To continue the swimming pool analogy, if I go swimming I'd much rather mess around and play with the kids or whiz down the flumes. The alternative is to take it terribly seriously and swim up and down, length after length, which isn't a lot of fun. It's also quite blinkered – you can't see a lot doing front crawl, except for water. It's also very solitary – you make no connection with anyone else, apart from the odd collision with passing playmakers. Both prayer and worship can be like doing lengths or they can be playful. In the end I splash around a lot in the deep end too, do a few lengths without overdoing it, play around some more, and leave feeling refreshed rather than exhausted.

Arthur Pedlar, a super British auguste clown and holy fool, also created a whiteface character called Arturo a few years ago, largely because he feared that the whiteface clown was dying out and we needed to be reminded of him. With his whiteface working to my auguste we've done a couple of sketches about prayer and play and their connections.

The first was done in a service in a Big Top, so we used as a basis an old clown circus routine. The basic plot is that the auguste comes in and starts to play a musical instrument, only to be stopped in his tracks by Whiteface who puts an end to all this noise and nonsense by maintaining the house rules that, 'You can't play here'. He grabs the instrument and strides off. Auguste then produces another instrument from about his person, looks at the floor where he's standing, and with wonderful clown logic decides that Whiteface didn't say he couldn't play over there, on the other side of the ring. Over he goes, and we start all over again. They go through a whole succession of instruments before they finally finish.

Arthur and I followed that basic scenario, although we reversed it a bit because it was me as auguste who kept making the entrances while he remained in the ring and in charge. It was the beginning of the service, and Arturo, who was naturally leading the worship, had asked for a moment of quiet, only to be interrupted by me charging in playing my trombone. I was summarily dispatched, Arturo apologized to the congregation for my behaviour, and then announced he was going to read some verses from scripture, only for me to come in and play a kazoo on the other side of the ring. Again I was banished from the ring with the words, 'You can't play here, you can't play there, you can't play anywhere!', ringing in my ears. Arturo then decided that perhaps we'd better start with a prayer, and made the time-honoured invitation to the congregation, 'Let us pray!' In I charged for a final time, blasting out 'When all the saints'. When Arturo complained, I reminded him that he'd said, Let us play. He denied it and corrected me, but then I suggested that it's the same thing anyway. After a brief exchange of views that reflect much of this chapter, Arturo complained that my music was awful, which indeed it was – I'm pretty hopeless at the trombone! But then I said his prayers were pretty awful too, and that just as we can't always get the tune right, so we can't always get the words right, but that at least in play you're always in with a chance. I then proffered him a half-size saxophone that I'd hidden in one of my cavernous pockets, and told him to try praying with that. He played it beautifully (it is his!) and we turned together to go out. The final punchline before we disappeared was mine. I turned and smiled, exclaiming to the congregation, 'Who says you can't pray here?!' It worked well and it set the playful and prayerful tone for the rest of the service.

The other routine we did was also at the beginning of a service, straight after the first hymn. Arthur wasn't in whiteface costume, just in whiteface character and mode! I wandered to the chancel step, happily and somewhat dreamily blowing bubbles. Suddenly Arthur stood up, all suited and booted in his Sunday best, wagging his finger at me in noisy protest that I was spoiling the service, that this was childish nonsense, and that this was the house of God – all that sort of thing! This was the first time I ever used bubbles as a way of offering up prayers, though I've used them a lot since then as my way of doing intercessions, using very few words. They provide a focus for prayer and it is their fragility that is so powerful. Each bubble becomes a vehicle for our prayers, and I always commend that as each bubble bursts, we should know that our prayers are heard.

Anyway, on that first occasion I hadn't worked all that out. Nevertheless I explained to Arthur the basis of it, and there is no doubt that there is something quite captivating about bubbles, not least because they speak of our childhood. What followed was a rapid costume change as Arthur was persuaded to put on a clown coat and trousers, and a big coloured bow tie instead of his formal dark blue one. These garments of faith were followed by a wig on his head so that he could think with the mind of Christ, greasepaint on his eyes and lips so that he could see and speak of the things of God, a clown's nose so that he couldn't look down on other people, and finally clown boots so that he could the walk the way of God. Then he was ready to blow some bubbles himself, before climbing on to a miniature unicycle and riding up the aisle to pursue his pilgrimage further. Again it was a powerful beginning because it probably echoed the initial reaction of some of the congregation but it also reflected the journey they would all take during the service.

Every service should aim to take us on that kind of journey where we are taken out of ourselves to behold all things new. It's what I have to do every time I put my costume on. If I just go through the motions, wheel out things that I know have worked well before, and ignore the Holy Spirit tapping on my shoulder, then things aren't going to happen. But if I go for it as if for the first time, then I'm led to do and say things that surprise me, never mind the congregation. I'm sure that some ad-libbing is the work of the Spirit in the moment, just as it is promised in the Bible that we will be given the words when we need them so we're not to worry what to say. The best ad-libs then get logged in the memory banks in the hope that they might turn up the next time it's appropriate, or they become fixtures in the story, another punchline. There are times in the Anglican Church when you need to break out of the mould, not use all the words available, and inject or allow spontaneity. That's not to say that we must be burdened with endless extempore prayers that burble round in circles and have their own formalized structures and wording – they're always the same, there must be a book of them somewhere, probably called, 'Lord, it's just . . .'! There are times, for instance, when at the beginning of the Eucharistic Prayer the priest says, 'The Lord is here', and the congregation dutifully reply in bold print rather than bold faith, 'His Spirit is with us', that I then want to add, 'Oh no he isn't!' It would be worth doing if I could be sure that the congregation would respond in great mirth and faith, 'Oh yes he is!', for then we really could go on to lift up our hearts as we are next bidden. Of course his Spirit is with us, we just have to know it in our hearts rather than merely assent to it with our lips.

In all worship we have to go for it rather than go through the motions, and that's true for those leading worship as much as for those who have turned up, young and old alike, and are sitting patiently in the pews, waiting for something to happen. Worship shouldn't be a spectator sport in that sense, for we all have to be involved. Thus a jolly romp through the choir's repertoire doesn't do a lot for me. Having worked alongside and tangled with a great number of choirs and music groups, I have no doubt that some of them should be banished from our churches until they learn to take themselves less seriously and discover that God isn't totally dependent on their musical virtuosity to make his will, purpose and love known to all people. Some of them are an arrogant lot, and extraordinarily patronizing! Good music and good choirs take us on spiritual journeys, they can uplift and inspire and take us into the moment. Congregations need to belt out a few good hymns and songs – they're very important to worship. By all means let's have action songs, if only so that we can all make fools of ourselves in the process. But let's do it all playfully.

There are some churches where it is only too obvious that the injunction, just like Arturo's, is that we can neither play nor pray here. You could write it up above the porch, 'Abandon hope all ye who enter here'! Worship that doesn't allow for laughter and tears misses a very important dimension. Church buildings that have never witnessed the sound of laughter or tears have not fulfilled their function. Laughter for me is the purest form of praise, while tears open us up to the promptings of the Spirit and the comfort of the Father. I'm not recommending that we become emotional wrecks every week, or that leaders of worship dabble in emotional hype, but we must be prepared to be moved, in every sense of the word. We are enjoined to love the Lord our God with all our heart, with all our mind, with all our strength and all our soul, and that's all I'm saying really! It's all of ourselves that must be involved in worship. Worship shouldn't be a clever set of mind games, though the readings may contain riddles aplenty. If there is story and laughter and symbol and sacrament and song, then all of ourselves will be involved. The clown teases and tempts us to be foolish enough to come out to pray, and those are some of the best things he has at his disposal as well as the things he himself enjoys most of all.

Meanwhile let's open our churches to all sorts of events. Before the advent of church halls and functional buildings, the church was where the people gathered. Let's use those serried pews for concerts and comedies and plays and pantomimes; or move all the chairs to the side and dance and eat and drink and party, confident that the one accused of being a drunkard and a friend of sinners is there in the midst. And the next day we can return to normal, whatever that is, just as those who celebrated the Feast of Fools did. Or we can do it again! In the end we come back to the worship of God in recognizable ways. But we have also to recognize that the concerts and plays and all the arts might also be offered as worship in themselves. I know that a lot of people in the past have seen my performance as worship in itself, just as Giovanni's act certainly was. Wouldn't it be wonderful if our churches became known as places of pleasure and leisure where all those who are heavy-burdened can come and rest, where people can come simply to enjoy themselves and to be themselves, and where 'Let us Play' is writ large above the door?

8

Playing the Fool

I think one of the reasons why people don't take the Church seriously is precisely because it takes itself too much so. The more it tries to be terribly meaningful, the more it loses sight of its true meaning; the more it tries to be really relevant, the more irrelevant it becomes. The dynamic of comedy is that the harder you try to be funny, the less funny it becomes, and we can all learn from that. Christianity isn't a serious business. Churches become graveyards, places for the grave and serious, if that happens, and graveyards sadly don't speak of resurrection – they just speak sadly! And the more the Church is seen as a business, the less Christ-like it surely becomes. Of course the Church and its churches must be efficient and organized and answer all its letters, but increasingly the Church and many of its churches are seen as vast and impersonal money-making enterprises staffed by people who serve the organization but not the people for whom the organization was created in the first place. I know one vicar who doesn't like working evenings or weekends, though he expects his congregation to. As I've travelled round, a number of parish vicars have despaired of the new young and not so young breed of curate who comes for interview with a whole agenda of things he isn't prepared to do, times he isn't prepared to work, and the absolutely crucial things which are, of course, to do with his accommodation. I remember being amazed at the quite matter-of-fact way that a hospital chaplain told me that of course he only worked thirty-seven and a half hours a week because that is what he was paid for. Fool that I am, I thought we were all called to serve God in a full-time capacity, at all times and in all places, and sometimes at the most ungodly hours! Where's the sense of vocation and of service, never mind the love?

There is that old saying that God loved the world so much that he didn't send a committee – now that's a good punchline! But the Church of England, for instance – with all its synods and committees and subcommittees and canon laws and subsection Cs and its mountains of paperwork – just staggers from pillar to post under the weight of its bureaucracy. The other Churches are no doubt just as bad. I sometimes wonder whether it's all done as a kind of glorified window dressing to persuade people that we're doing things properly and thus have to be taken seriously. It's at the heart of everything, isn't it!

It's the same with evangelism. In the USA especially, we have the awful prospect of all those fiercely intense and money-grabbing television evangelists, who remain more famous for their fraud and hypocrisy than for the gospel, and who demand to be taken seriously for their propensity for credit card salvation. But in the UK there is this strange version of evangelism that leads very severe and usually oddly-dressed people to stand on street corners and in shopping malls, and just shout very loudly and often very accusingly at passers-by. Rather like an Englishman talking to a foreigner who speaks no English at all, the evangelists think that if they talk loudly enough and slowly enough and, most importantly, for long enough, somehow they'll be understood in the end, that the message will get through! What nonsense! You have to speak the same language if you're going to share the journey of faith.

But this is the whiteface Church, bossy and pompous, fussy and frustrated, self-seeking and self-serving, thinking it knows best and will thus do everything itself in its own way, which is of course the right way and the only way. Jesus called the whitefaces 'whitewashed tombs' – a good description for the church of the graveyard! Whiteface needs the entrance of an auguste otherwise he'll never get his come-uppance – which I guess is where I come in, but it's also where Jesus came in.

I think the Church has to learn to play the fool and give up its pretensions to playing things straight. The Church, and thus all churches and all Christians, has to be true to itself, and true to the God it not only believes in but claims to represent. Only then can it be a truth-teller with any credibility and audience, never mind the Truth-teller to the world. The Church must be the vulnerable lover, open to all, undemanding, playful and embracing. The Church must learn to live on the edges as well as on the edge, on the outside, taking risks, tested by the wilderness, a prophetic voice, never quite belonging, in the world but not of it. The Church must learn to sing and laugh and cry, a minstrel Church who speaks of mysteries and mystery, in riddles and in verse. The Church must learn to tell its story, to be the story, to let people see it for themselves, to let the world get the joke. The Church like the clown must be irrepressible and indefatigable, a symbol of hope and endless possibilities as well as eternal life, led by the Spirit of playfulness, spontaneously seizing the moment, second by second, never missing a trick or an opportunity, playing with failure, falling and rising, getting it hopelessly wrong and gloriously right. Then there is laughter, then there is true joy, then the Good News will be heard throughout the land, for the gospel, like the Clown, is priceless.

Now that's a foolish vision if ever there was one, but

wouldn't it be good if even some of it happened! Meanwhile, as in all good clown routines, we have whiteface churches alongside auguste ones and tramp ones, and at their best they all work well together. But they need to keep the twinkle in their eye and let their imagination run riot, and bounce off us and each other in a happy anarchy. We just need to play together.

If the Church can learn to play the fool, then we'll suddenly discover that things have changed, that other people not only recognize the wisdom of the fool but seek it out and listen to it too. I've just received a letter from a woman who came to the Ely Diocesan Conference. She wrote, 'This weekend through you the Holy Spirit opened my mind, heart and eyes to see Christ. It is such a revelation. All those hundreds who came to hear him. I didn't question it and yet the Christ I thought I knew could never have captured them like that. Christ the Clown could. The ride into Jerusalem, "the stones would cry out", I heard you/Him shout it – and the laughter. Thank you. I begin to understand.'

I suppose all I've done throughout my ministry and most of my life is to pursue the vision and follow Christ's example, exactly as I am called and bidden to do. If by sharing my story and trying to articulate that vision, it's encouraged you, then my work is done. All you have to do now is take a deep breath, laugh out loud, go for it, and pray and play the fool! If it can happen to me, it can happen to anyone – and that includes you!